REVISED EDITION

Filling Out
FORMS

New Readers Press

Filling Out Forms
ISBN 978-1-56420-400-4

Copyright © 2007, 1986, 1979 New Readers Press
New Readers Press
Division of ProLiteracy Worldwide
1320 Jamesville Avenue, Syracuse, New York 13210
www.newreaderspress.com

Printed in the United States of America
9 8 7 6 5 4 3 2 1

All proceeds from the sale of New Readers Press materials
support literacy programs in the United States and worldwide.

Writer: Anne Martin
Developmental Editor: Terrie Lipke
Design and Production Manager: Andrea Woodbury
Designer: Carolyn Boehmer
Production Specialist: Maryellen Casey

Contents

To the Student   4

1   **Before You Start**   5

2   **Personal Information**   11
personal data sheet   library card application

3   **Banking and Money**   21
account application   personal check
deposit slip   postal money order
withdrawal slip   checking account register

4   **Consumer Concerns**   33
mail offers   credit card application
catalog order form   pre-approved credit application
warranty/registration   loan application
merchandise return form   rental agreement
customer survey   lease application

5   **Education and Employment**   47
course registration form
job application
W-4 form
unemployment insurance application

6   **Health Care**   58
medical history
patient billing and insurance information form
medical insurance enrollment form
government health care form

7   **Driving and Automobile Insurance**   72
driver's license application
vehicle registration application
auto insurance claim form

8   **Citizenship and Voting**   84
customs declaration   passport application
naturalization application   voter registration

Resources   95

To the Student

Shopping online, depositing money into your bank account, registering to vote, and signing up for a yoga class—what do these things have in common? The answer is—filling out forms.

You fill out forms at home, at school, and at work. Some forms are on paper. Some forms are on the Internet, and you use a computer to fill them out. But the process for filling out forms is the same.

This book will teach you four basic steps to filling out forms. You can follow the steps for any type of form. Learning about forms will help you learn practical skills that you can use day after day.

At the beginning of each lesson there is a list of key words. Go over the key words list and see how many of these terms you already know. Don't worry if you are not familiar with all the words. They will be defined or explained in the lesson. You may learn other new words as you read the lesson. Add these words to your key words list.

A list of forms at the beginning of the lesson tells you which forms you will practice filling out. Do you have any of these types of forms at home? Do you need to fill out one of these forms? If so, you may want to bring the form to class for more practice.

Some forms ask for personal or private information. If you do not want to share this information with your teacher or your classmates, just leave those lines blank. Write a note to yourself so you will remember what to write if you need to enter that information on a real form.

Forms are all around you. You can find forms at work, at the super-market, at local businesses, and on the Internet. The more forms you practice filling out, the easier it will be for you to fill out the forms you need. The Resources section in the back of this book lists some places where you can find common forms. Your teacher can also help you to find forms for practice.

The lessons in this book can help you deal with many different types of forms. And when you know how to fill out forms, you can take care of business and have fun, too.

Before You Start

KEY WORDS

online forms

download

submit

electronic filing

application

mandatory

optional

eligible

gender

documents

valid

fine print

witness

enclose

GETTING READY

Forms are part of everyday life. We fill out forms at home, at work, at the bank, at the store, etc. This book will help you understand and fill out some common forms. Here are some things you need to think about when you are getting ready to fill out a form.

How do you get the form?

You may get a form in person when you go to an office. Some forms come in the mail. You may find or request a form on a computer web site. Some forms can be filled out using a computer. They are called **online forms.** Some forms can be printed out from the computer and then filled out on paper. Or you can fill out forms online and then print them out.

Many agencies and companies put forms on their web sites. You may need to **download** the form (get the computer file for the form). You can print out a copy. Or you can **submit** (send in) the form online. Filling out and submitting a form online is sometimes called **electronic filing.** Some tax forms, order forms, and **applications** can be completed this way. An application is a form that you use to ask for something, like a job or a bank loan.

Make a copy of any form you fill out. Keep it for your records.

Do you need to fill out the form?

Some forms are **mandatory** (required). That means you *must* fill out the form. For example, you must fill out a Customs Declaration form when you arrive in the U.S. This is mandatory for everyone: visitors, students, immigrants, and U.S. citizens.

Other forms are **optional** (not required). You may choose to fill out an optional form, or you may choose not to fill it out. Some examples of optional forms are magazine subscription cards, credit card applications, and opinion surveys.

FILLING OUT THE FORM

Follow these four steps to fill out any form.

1. **Read the form and the instructions.** Collect information you need to complete the form. If you don't understand the form, ask someone for help.

2. **Fill out the form.** If the form is complicated, use a copy of it to fill out a first draft.

3. **Read the completed form and check your answers.** Correct errors. Make sure all information has been filled in. If it is a first draft, copy your answers onto the final form.

4. **Sign and submit the form.** Sign the form. Write the date if you need to. Follow the instructions to submit the form.

Let's look closely at each step.

STEP 1:

Read the Form and the Instructions

Do you have all of the information you need? Make a list and collect the information.

Here are some examples of information you may be asked for on a form.

Most forms ask you to fill out this information:
- Name
- Address

Some forms ask for contact information:
- Phone number(s)
- Fax number
- E-mail address

Some forms ask for more personal information:
- Social Security number
- Sex or gender (male/female)
- Marital status
- Country of birth
- Citizenship

Forms may also ask for detailed information:
- Residency status
- Family information (number of children, parents' names, etc.)
- Education information
- Health history
- Financial information
- Product information (such as a registration number)

This book will help you understand what a form is asking for. And it will help you to find and fill in the correct information.

You may need to fill out a form quickly, for example, to get emergency medical help at a hospital. It is important to have certain information with you or to know where you can find it quickly (e.g., your medical insurance ID number, Social Security number, or basic medical information).

<u>Collecting Supporting Material</u> Sometimes a form asks you for other information. The form may ask for **documents** or **supporting material.** These are papers that show specific information such as a receipt that shows proof of purchase or your birth certificate that shows proof of age. If supporting material is required, submit a copy of the documents along with the form. If you submit the form in person, bring the original documents with you.

These are examples of supporting material or documents you may be asked to provide.

- Proof of identity: To prove who you are, you need your signature and your photo. Your passport has both your signature and your photo. It is **valid** (legally accepted) proof of identity. A driver's license or a school or work ID card may also be proof of identity.

- Proof of age: Your birth certificate or other record of birth is proof of your age. Passports and most driver's licenses show your birth date, too. Other documents that prove your age include school, church, or marriage records, and military papers.

- Citizenship or immigration status: People not born in the U.S. may need a passport, birth or naturalization certificate, green card (U.S. work permit), or report of birth from a consulate.

- Other supporting material you may be asked to provide: Some forms require a copy of your Social Security card, copies of documents (such as your marriage certificate or divorce decree), school transcripts, health records, proof of purchase, proof of payment, death certificate for a parent or family member, etc.

STEP 2: Fill Out the Form

Before you begin to write, scan the form and instructions one more time. Are there instructions for filling out the form? Read them carefully. For example, if the instructions say, "use black ink only," get a black pen.

Read instructions or labels that tell you where to write. Notice spaces where you are told not to write anything. These spaces are marked with phrases like "Do not write below this line" or "For office use only."

Look for instruction words that tell you what to write, where to write, and how to write it. Here are some general guidelines:

- Follow instructions about writing tools (for example, *use ink, pen, pencil*, etc.) and style (*print, use **block letters,** capital letters, sign*, etc.).
  Block letters: THOMPSON ROAD

- For handwritten forms, use a blue or black ballpoint pen. For some forms, like a standardized test, you may be told to use pencil. Print the information. Do not use cursive handwriting.
  Printing: Thompson Road
  Cursive handwriting: *Thompson Road*

- Some forms must be typed or filled out on a computer. These online forms usually have boxes that you type information into.

  Lydia Suranyi

- Sometimes the form has small boxes to fill in or check. Use X or ✓ to mark a box.
  Check one box:　☒ Yes　　☐ No

- Do not print your signature. When you sign your name, write it in cursive writing.
  Signature: *Marianne F. Wentworth*

STEP 3: Read the Completed Form and Check Your Answers

After you have filled out the form, read it over to make sure you are finished. Ask these questions:

- Did you follow all of the instructions, including any **fine print?** Fine print is detailed explanations in small type. Reread them to be sure.

- Have you filled in everything that is required? Check for any blank spaces.

- Did you make any mistakes? Correct your spelling.

- Are your answers easy to read? Make sure everything is readable.

- Have you answered as accurately as you can? Check your facts.

- Are you ready to submit the form?

STEP 4: Sign and Submit the Form

Some forms require you to sign your name at the end. You may also be asked to write the date. When you sign your name or write your signature, you are making a promise. First, you promise that you are who you say you are. Second, you promise that the information you have provided is true and accurate. Third, you promise to agree to any conditions or requirements stated on the form.

In some cases, there are penalties if you do not tell the truth on a form. For example, you may be fined, suspended from school or work, or not allowed to get a certain job if you are not truthful.

Sign your name in cursive writing the way you always sign it. If there is a space for the date, write the date that you are completing the form. You may need to have a **witness** when you sign your name. A witness is someone who watches you sign the form and then signs next to your signature. Sometimes you need to sign at the time you hand in the form.

Before you submit the form, make a final check. Have you completed the entire form? Have you signed the form? Have you included required materials? Now you're ready to submit the form. There are three ways to submit a form: by mail, in person, and by computer. Read the instructions to find out which way to submit the form.

<u>Submitting a form by mail</u> Sometimes a pre-addressed envelope is provided. A pre-addressed envelope has the address printed on it. Other times you need to prepare an envelope. Use an envelope that is big enough for your form and any other material you need to include.

The instructions will indicate the mailing address. If no envelope is provided, copy the address carefully onto the center of an envelope. Write your name and return address on the upper left corner of the envelope. **Enclose** the form (put it in the envelope) along with any required materials. Seal the envelope.

Does the envelope need a stamp? A postage-paid envelope has a permit stamped on it that says "No Postage Required." Some envelopes say "Place Stamp Here." Be sure to put on a stamp if it is needed. If you do not know how much postage to use, take the envelope to a post office.

An envelope with your address printed on it and a stamp on it is called a self-addressed stamped envelope (SASE). If you are expecting a reply, you may be asked to enclose an SASE.

<u>Submitting a form in person</u> If the instructions say to submit the form *in person,* take the form to the office. You may have been told where to submit the form when you picked it up. Or the instructions may tell you the address of where to go. Bring required supporting material with you in case you are asked to show it.

<u>Submitting a form by computer</u> Follow the instructions on the web site for submitting an online form. Enter the requested information very carefully. Reread the form and the instructions to be sure it is completed correctly. When you are ready, press *enter* or click on the *submit* button, according to the instructions. You may receive a reply message. Read the message to see if your form was successfully submitted.

REVIEW & DISCUSS

Answer the questions.

1. Describe the four steps to filling out a form. _____

   _____

   _____

   _____

2. Name three types of supporting material. _____

   _____

3. List three ways to submit a form. _____

   _____

4. Have you filled out any forms? Talk to your classmates about your experiences filling out forms.

Personal Information

KEY WORDS

applicant

surname

spouse

dependent

permanent
address

mailing
address

residence

e-mail

Social Security
number

occupation

Forms:

• personal data sheet

• library card application

FILLING OUT BASIC INFORMATION

Many forms ask for basic information about you such as your name, address, and phone number. Here are some terms and descriptions that will help you fill out forms correctly.

Name

Almost every form asks for your name. Forms may ask for your name in many different ways:

Student	Patient	Claimant
Customer	Applicant	Insured
Employee	Registrant	Account holder

Each term relates to a specific type of form. For example, a medical form may use *patient*. Terms for names often end in *–ant,* and they may be related to another word on the form. For example, an **applicant** is someone who is *applying* or who is filling out an *application.*

Forms usually require your first name and last name. Sometimes they ask for them in reverse order. In reverse order, your last name goes before your first name. Some forms ask for your middle name or middle initial (MI). Your middle initial is the first letter of your middle name.

Most forms need your *formal* name. This is your full name as it appears on your birth certificate and other legal documents. You might have a nickname or a shortened version of your name that you use with friends and family. Some forms may ask for your *preferred* name. That is the name you would like people to use, informally. In that case, you can write your nickname.

Special situations A married woman should use her own first name. In many cultures, a woman who marries takes her husband's **surname** (last name), but not always. In the U.S., some women choose to keep their maiden names (their family surnames). Some women use both maiden name and husband's last name, sometimes with a hyphen in between. In some cultures, a woman's last name changes in another way to show that she is married. For example, Maria Gomez became Maria Gomez de Castellas after she married Pedro Castellas.

Print your name clearly. If you need to fill it in several times, write it the same way every time. For example, on some travel forms your name must exactly match the name on your passport.

Two-person or family forms will have two or more lines for names (for example, a joint banking account form or a family medical history form).

_____Anwar_____ and _____Fatma Abed_____

Mr. and Mrs. _____Cha_____ _____Xiong_____

and child (children) _____Tricia_____ , _____David_____ , _____

Other names a form may require:

- **Spouse** (husband or wife)
- **Dependent** (someone that you support, usually a child)
- Parent or guardian
- Mother's maiden name
- Title, such as Junior (Jr.), Senior (Sr.), or Doctor (Dr.)

DISCUSS & PRACTICE

Here are some names from a variety of cultural backgrounds. A person's name often reflects his or her cultural heritage, but not always.

Alberto de la Rosa	Ji Myong Wang	Lucilla Pieta
Mohamad bin Sharif	Jessica Wilton	Dakota Blackfoot

Does your name reflect your cultural origin or family background? Explain to your class the origin of your name.

Practice writing your name.

First _____ Middle Initial _____ Last Name _____

Last Name _____ First Name _____ Middle Name _____

Circle: Mr. Mrs. Miss Ms. Dr. Name _____

_____ _____ _____
(First name)   (MI)   (Last name)

Address

There are two kinds of addresses you may be asked to write. They are your **permanent address** and your **mailing address.** Your *permanent* address, or **residence,** is where you usually live. If you are on a trip or away at school, it is your home (or legal) address.

Your *mailing* address is where you receive your mail. Your mailing address may be the address of a building (for example, the apartment or house where you live). Or it may be a post office (PO) box. It may also be a rural route (RR) number or a military address (APO or FPO).

Your permanent address and mailing address may be the same or may be different. Be sure to read the form carefully and write the correct address. If a form asks for both your permanent address and mailing address, and they are the same, write *SAME* in the second space.

Know these terms when writing your address in the U.S.:

- Street: This is the building or house number and street. You may live on a street, an avenue, a road, a boulevard, etc. Some street addresses include a direction (e.g., Northwest or NW).

- Apartment: A form may say *Apartment Number* or *APT.* If you live in a building with more than one unit, write your apartment or unit number clearly. It may be a number or a number and a letter, for example, Apt. 201 or #4F.

- City: This is the community (city, town, or village) where you live. For a mailing address, it is the name of the place where you receive your mail.

- State: You may use the two-letter postal abbreviation if you know it. For example, New York=NY, Colorado=CO. If you do not know the abbreviation, write out the name. If there is a blank space for only two letters, you will need the state's abbreviation. You can call your local post office to get it.

- Zip code: U.S. zip codes have at least five digits (e.g., 10001). Some mail has a nine-digit zip code, called a zip plus four (ZIP + 4®). The zip plus four is written like this: 10001–4321. If you need the nine-digit zip and you do not know it, call your local post office.

- Country: Some forms ask for the country. For an address in the United States, write the abbreviation *U.S.* or *USA.*

Sometimes the address line or space is very small. Print carefully, and use abbreviations when necessary. For example:

Road = Rd.	Avenue = Ave.	North = N
Street = St.	Boulevard = Blvd.	Southeast = SE

On some legal forms, for example, a voter registration form, you may need to write the county you live in. A county is a division within a state. There may be many different cities or towns in a county.

PRACTICE

Here are some examples of how to fill out address lines on forms:

Street _1234 Main St._ _Apt. 3C_

City _Sunnyvale_   State _CA_   Zip code _94088_

STREET											APT						
1	2	3	4		M	A	I	N		S	T		A	P	T		3	C		
S	U	N	N	Y	V	A	L	E		C	A		9	4	0	8	8			

CITY   STATE   ZIP

Now practice writing your own address.

PERMANENT ADDRESS

STREET ADDRESS _____ APARTMENT NO. _____

CITY and STATE _____ ZIP CODE _____

MAILING ADDRESS (if different)

STREET ADDRESS _____ APARTMENT NO. _____

CITY and STATE _____ ZIP CODE _____

Street Address   Apt.

City   State   Zip

Phone Number

Many forms ask for your telephone number. A form may say *phone number, phone no., Tel.,* or *Ph.* Write your home phone number. Sometimes the form will ask for more specific phone information. Here are some examples:

- Phone (Daytime or Day)
- Phone (Evening or Eve.)
- Tel (Work or W)
- Tel (Home or H)
- Extension (Ext.)
- Cell phone (Cell)

A phone number in the U.S. is a three-digit area code (AC) and a seven-digit number. For example (111) 555-1000 shows the area code in parentheses then the seven-digit number. Your work number may also have an extension, for example, (111) 555-1000, ext. 222. If you do not have a work phone, draw a line through that space.

Some forms require a phone number. For example, when you submit a job application, someone may need to contact you about the job opening. When you submit a medical form, the office or doctor needs a contact phone number in case of an emergency. It is important to have a way for someone to reach you by telephone.

PRACTICE

Now practice writing your phone number.

Phone: (_____) _____ – _____

Tel.: (Area Code first) _____

Phone (H) (_____) _____ (W) (_____) _____ ext. _____

<u>Other contact information</u> Some forms have spaces for other contact information. These are usually optional.

- Fax: Most businesses, and some individuals, have a fax (facsimile) machine to receive and send documents. Draw a line through the space if you do not have a fax number.

- E-mail: Many forms have a line for your **e-mail** address. E-mail is electronic mail sent and received by computer. Draw a line through the space if you do not use e-mail.

Dates

Forms may require your date of birth, the date of application, dates of employment, or the date of an accident. Use numbers to write the day and year. The month may be a number or a word. Read and follow the instructions on the form. This is how to write dates:

- Day: This is a number from 1 to 31. You may have two spaces or two lines. Put a *0* in the first space for any number below 10. For example, *7* may be written as *07.*

- Month: Sometimes you can write out the name of the month. Many forms only have space for a number. January is month 1, and the months are numbered in order, through December, which is 12. If there are two spaces, put a *0* before the single-digit number. For example, *August* is *08.*

- Year: The year may be written as two or four digits. For example, *2006* may be written *06,* and *1998* may be written *98.*

On U.S. forms, always write the month, day, then year, unless the instructions say otherwise. Some forms have slashes (/) or hyphens (-) between the numbers. For example, *August 7, 2006* can be written as *08/07/06* or *8-7-06.*

Sometimes an abbreviation appears under the line to show you how to write the date. For example, YY/MM/DD indicates that you write the year (two digits), month (two digits), day (two digits), with slashes between the numbers.

Some forms have a line for you to write the date next to your signature. Unless the form specifies, you may write the date in any way. For example, you can write November 12, 2006, 11/12/06, or 11-12-06.

PRACTICE

Practice writing your date of birth.

Month ___ ___ Day ___ ___ Year ___ ___ ___ ___

DD/MM/YYYY _____

Practice writing today's date.

Today's Date: _____

Month ___ ___ Day ___ ___ Year ___ ___

YY/MM/DD _____

Social Security Number

Many forms ask for your **Social Security number.** This is your number with the U.S. Social Security Administration. You will need a Social Security number in order to open a bank account, to apply for government services, or to get a job. The number has nine digits, written in three groups. For example, Social Security numbers look like this: *999-88-7777.* Some forms use an abbreviation like *Soc. Sec. No.* or *SSN.*

The hyphens (or spaces) are important. Be sure to write all the numbers in the correct order. If you do not have a Social Security number, see Section 5 for more information.

PRACTICE

Do you know your Social Security number? Practice writing your Social Security number on a separate piece of paper. When you're done, shred or tear up the paper.

Personal Information

Some forms ask for personal information, such as your age, your sex, or your marital status. Other forms ask for physical features like your height, weight, or the color of your eyes. For example, a driver's license application asks you to describe several physical features.

Age Your date of birth indicates your age. Some forms, for example a health form, may ask for your age in years. Write your age as of your last birthday. Do not provide your age unless it is required.

Some forms ask for you to choose an age range. Check the range that includes your current age.

Consumer Alert

Your Social Security number is private. Keep your card in a safe place with your other important papers. Do not carry it with you unless you need to show it to an employer or service provider. Be very careful about giving out your Social Security number. If a form asks for your number, find out why it is needed and how it will be used.

<u>Sex or Gender</u> Indicate whether you are male or female. Some forms require you to write or circle *M* (male) or *F* (female).

<u>Marital Status</u> If a form requires your marital status, tell whether you are married or single. Some forms include other choices such as divorced (your marriage has been legally ended), separated (you are still legally married but not living together), or widowed (your spouse has died).

<u>Personal Characteristics</u>

- Height: In the U.S., give your height in feet and inches. Use ' for feet and " for inches. For example, if you are five feet and nine inches tall, write *5'9"*.

- Weight: In the U.S., give your weight in pounds (lbs.). If you weigh 165 pounds, print *165 lbs.*

- Color of eyes (eye color): Use a one- or two- word answer. Here are some examples: brown, blue, gray, blue-green, hazel.

- Color of hair (hair color): Use one or two words. Examples: blonde, black, brown, light brown, gray, auburn, white.

PRACTICE

1. Write your height in feet and inches. _____

2. Write your weight in pounds. _____

3. Write your eye color. _____

4. Write your hair color. _____

Other Categories of Personal Information

Some forms ask for information about your **occupation** or profession (what you do for work), your place of work, citizenship, your nationality, or ethnic group.

- Occupation: What type of work do you do? Write the job that you do.

- Place of Work: Where do you work? There may be a line for the name of the business or for the business name and address.

- Citizenship: Are you a U.S. citizen? If you are a U.S. citizen by birth or naturalization, write *U.S.* If you are not, write the name of the country in which you are a citizen.

- Nationality: Your nationality tells what country you were born in or belong to. Use the word that describes the people of your country. For example, if you were born in France, your nationality is French. If you were born in Nigeria, your nationality is Nigerian. U.S. citizens write *U.S.* on the line.

- Ethnic Group: What is your race? Some forms ask for your ethnicity or ethnic group. It is usually optional. Census forms (population surveys) request ethnic group information. If the question is optional, you do not have to answer. Usually you choose your ethnicity from a list. Some examples are Asian, Black, Caucasian, Hispanic, or Eastern European.

PRACTICE

A personal data sheet is a place to keep track of information about yourself. As you work through this book, you may want to create your own personal data sheet with information you use to fill out forms. Fill out this form to practice writing information about yourself.

Personal Data Sheet

Name: _____
               first   middle   last

Address: _____

_____

Phone: home (_____) _____   work (_____) _____

Date of Birth: _____ / _____ / _____   Sex: _____ M _____ F

Social Security Number: _____ – _____ – _____

Hair Color: _____   Eye Color: _____

Occupation: _____

Place of Work: _____

Citizenship: _____

Nationality: _____

Ethnic Group: _____

Read the library card application, and answer the questions below it. Then fill out the form.

Pleasantville Public Library   **Library Card Application**

Please print. Submit form at Pleasantville Public Library. Bring photo ID.

Name (Last, First, MI): _____

Parent/Guardian (if under 18): _____

Address _____
        No.   Street   Apt. #

_____
        City   State   Zip

E-mail Address: _____

> Providing the following voluntary information will help us better plan our programs and services. This information is confidential.
> ☐ Senior Citizen (62+)   ☐ Adult (18–62)
> ☐ Young Adult (12–17)   ☐ Child (under 12)
> Sex   ☐ Male ☐ Female

Would you like to be on the library mailing list?   ☐ Yes ☐ No

Signature _____ Date _____

Parent/Guardian _____ Date _____

---

1. How do you submit the form? _____

2. Do you need to show ID? _____

3. Do you need to give your date of birth? _____

4. Is any information optional? _____

5. What instructions are given about how to fill out the form?

   _____

   _____

6. Do you write your name in reverse order?

   _____

7. Who needs to have a parent or guardian sign?

   _____

8. Are you required to write your age? _____

GOOD INFORMATION HABITS

It is important to protect yourself by keeping your personal information safe. Here are some rules.

1. Do not give more information on a form than is required.

   • Do not give out your Social Security number unless it is necessary. If you do have to provide the number (for example, to your employer or your bank), make sure it will be kept confidential.

   • Do not give out contact information unless it is required. When you write your phone number on a form, you give the company permission to call you.

   • Do not give financial information unless it is required.

   • Do not give anyone your bank account or credit card Personal Identification Number (PIN) or password. Choose a PIN or password carefully. Do not use obvious words or numbers such as your birth date or name.

2. Keep copies of forms you have filled out. That way you have a record of information you gave a company, organization, or office.

3. Be sure a company or organization is reliable before you supply personal information. A good company will tell you how it protects your privacy.

4. Use credit cards carefully. Give the account number or card only to reliable companies or organizations.

5. Protect your documents. Keep your passport, birth certificate, naturalization papers, etc., in a safe place at home and when you travel.

6. Do not carry more cards or personal information than necessary. Do not carry your Social Security card with you.

7. Dispose of unneeded information or forms carefully. When you throw away anything with personal information on it (e.g., old credit cards, bank statements, receipts, etc.), shred it or cut it up.

Banking and Money

KEY WORDS

account
ATM
interest
transactions
deposit
withdraw
write a check
endorse
direct deposit
personal
identification
number (PIN)
debit card
checkbook
overdrawn
insufficient
funds
payee
void
money order
check register
debit
credit
balance
statement
canceled check

Forms:

- account application
- deposit slip
- withdrawal slip
- personal check
- postal money order
- checking account register

OPENING A BANK ACCOUNT

Banks keep your money safe. When you put money in a bank for the first time, you fill out an application form to open an **account.** The bank holds your money in an account.

Choose a bank with a branch or local office near your home, school, or work. Banks have different services. Many have **ATMs** (automated teller machines), drive-up windows, safe-deposit boxes (for storing valuable items), and other services.

What kind of account do you need?

When you open an account, you will make some choices. Do you want a savings account or a checking account? A savings account helps you save money for the future. You earn **interest** on your savings. Interest is money the bank pays you for keeping your money there.

A checking account helps you pay bills. You can write checks to make payments. Some banks offer linked, or connected, savings and checking accounts. You can write checks, and the money that stays in the bank earns interest. Ask if you have to pay a fee or charge every month. Some accounts are free. And some banks charge you for each check you write.

There are many other types of bank accounts. A bank official will describe the types of accounts that are available so you can choose the account that is best for you.

How do you apply for an account?

The official will help you fill out an account application. If you are single, get an individual account. This is just in your name. A joint account is used by two people (for example, a married couple). Two names will be on the account and on the checks. Both people can use the account.

In some banks, the account application is only on the computer. The bank official will ask you questions and type the information into the computer or give you a form to fill out.

You need to sign the account application. Sign the form exactly the way you usually sign your name. This is your official signature. Also, you will be asked to provide personal identification: Social Security number, picture ID (such as your driver's license), another form of ID, or employment information. You may be asked to tell about other bank accounts you have had.

You have to put money in the bank to open your account. Ask the bank official to tell you the minimum, or smallest amount, you need.

REVIEW

Study the account application. Then answer the questions.

Account Application

Account type __passbook savings__   Amount of deposit ___$100.00___

Account Holder Information

Mr./Mrs./(Miss)/Ms./Dr.   First Name __Thuy__   MI __L__   Last Name __Nguyen__

Social Security Number __999-11-2222__   Date of Birth __06/04/87__

Mother's Maiden Name __Tran__

Home Phone __315-555-1199__   Work Phone __315-555-7654__

Employer's Name __Village Pharmacy__   Occupation __clerk__

Street Address __123 South Tulip Street__

City __Round Rock__   State __TX__   Zip Code __78664__

Mailing Address __same__

City _____   State _____   Zip Code _____

Length of Time at Current Address __3 years__

Driver's License State __TX__   Number __123 456 789__

Country of Citizenship __U.S.__

---

1. What type of account is the person applying for? _____

2. Is it an individual or joint account? _____

3. What ID or other information does the person provide?

   _____

4. How much money was put in to open the account? _____

5. Where does the person work? _____

Practice applying for a bank account. Fill out the basic information.

Account Application

Account type _____ Amount of deposit _____

Account Holder Information

Mr./Mrs./Miss/Ms./Dr.   First Name _____ MI _____ Last Name _____

Social Security Number _____ Date of Birth _____

Mother's Maiden Name _____

Home Phone _____ Work Phone _____

Employer's Name _____ Occupation _____

Street Address _____

City _____ State _____ Zip Code _____

Mailing Address _____

City _____ State _____ Zip Code _____

Length of Time at Current Address _____

Driver's License State _____ Number _____

Country of Citizenship _____

MAKING TRANSACTIONS

Banking activities are often called **transactions.** These are three of the most common transactions:

- **depositing** money (adding money to your account)
- **withdrawing** money (taking money out of your account)
- **writing a check** (making a payment by filling out a form that tells the bank to pay someone with money from your account)

Depositing Money

You can deposit checks or cash into your checking or savings account. You will need to fill out a deposit slip or ticket to put with your money. A deposit slip tells the bank how much money you want to put in your account. You can get a deposit slip from the back of your checkbook or at your bank. The slip in your checkbook already has your name and account number on it. If you get a deposit slip from the bank, fill in your name and account number. Then write the date of your deposit. Fill in the amount of cash you are depositing. Fill in the amount of each check you are depositing. Then add up the total and write it on the deposit slip.

If you are depositing a check and you would like some cash back, look for the line that says *Less cash* or *Less cash received.* Write the amount of cash you want. Then subtract it from the total of your deposit. The remaining amount is your *net* deposit, or the amount that will actually go into your account. Sign your name on the line that says *Sign here.*

Deposit money into your account at your bank or at an ATM. When you deposit a check written to you, like a paycheck, you need to **endorse** it (sign it on the back). Write your bank account number below your signature. Never endorse a check before you get to the bank. Anyone can cash an endorsed check.

Some employers offer **direct deposit** for paychecks. Your pay is electronically transferred into your account without a paper check. You will get a payment record from your employer telling you the date and the amount of the deposit.

REVIEW & PRACTICE

Study the deposit slip. Then answer the questions.

DEPOSIT TICKET

CHECKS AND OTHER ITEMS ARE RECEIVED FOR DEPOSIT SUBJECT TO THE PROVISIONS OF THE UNIFORM COMMERCIAL CODE OR ANY APPLICABLE COLLECTION AGREEMENT.

NAME __Thuy Nguyen__

ACCOUNT NO. __43-887589__

DATE __11/10/06__

DEPOSITS MAY NOT BE AVAILABLE FOR IMMEDIATE WITHDRAWAL

Thuy Nguyen
SIGN HERE FOR CASH RECEIVED (IF REQUIRED)

First Federal Savings & Loan Association New York, NY

CASH				
CHECKS	2 7	1	4	3
	5 0	0	0	
CHECK OR TOTAL FROM OTHER SIDE				
SUB TOTAL	3 2	1	4	3
LESS CASH RECEIVED	2 5	0	0	
$	2 9	6 . 4	3	

1. How many checks are listed? _____

2. What is the subtotal of the checks? _____

3. How much cash will the person receive? _____

4. What is the total deposit? _____

Fill out the deposit slip. You will deposit two checks. One is from your employer for $315.22, and one is from a friend for $20.85. You will take out $50 as cash received.

DEPOSIT

94-321555-01		DATE		
ACCOUNT NUMBER			DOLLARS	CENTS
		CASH		
DEPOSIT TO THE ACCOUNT OF:		**CHECKS** List separately and endorse each item		
_____				
_____				
SIGN HERE FOR CASH RECEIVED (IF REQUIRED)				
_____		Less cash		
Checks and other items are received for deposit subject to the provisions of the uniform commercial code or any applicable collection agreement.	**ABC** **BANK & TRUST**	**TOTAL**		

Withdrawing Money

When you withdraw money, you will get cash. You can withdraw money in person at your bank. Fill out a withdrawal slip to take money out of your savings account. You get a withdrawal slip at the bank. The withdrawal slip has lines for the date, account number, withdrawal amount, and your signature.

You can take money out of your checking account by writing a personal check. On the *Pay to* line, write *CASH*. When you get to the bank, fill in the amount in numbers and in words, and sign the check. Then turn the check over and endorse it. Sign on the line marked *Endorse here.* Your signature must match your name and signature on the front. Do not endorse the check before you get to the bank.

Another way to withdraw money is by using an ATM. Most banks have ATMs for use anytime. You must have an ATM card and a **personal identification number (PIN)** to use an ATM. Your bank or credit card company will give you a PIN. Use your ATM card or **debit card** and your PIN to withdraw money. A debit card withdraws money from your account for cash or to pay for purchases. The withdrawal is processed automatically, and you receive the cash and a receipt. To protect your account, do not let other people use your ATM card. Do not tell anyone your PIN.

You can also withdraw money in the form of traveler's checks. This is a safe way to carry money when you are away from home.

REVIEW & PRACTICE

Study the withdrawal slip. Then answer the questions.

WITHDRAWAL

43-887589
ACCOUNT NUMBER

$ 70.00
WITHDRAWAL AMOUNT

12/4/06
DATE

seventy and no/00 _____ DOLLARS
Please write amount in words

☑ Cash Withdrawal   ☐ Check Payable to: _____

☐ Transfer to Account # (s) _____

**First Federal Savings
& Loan Association
New York, NY**

Thuy Nguyen
SIGNATURE

_____
SIGNATURE

1. How much money was withdrawn? _____

2. Was the money withdrawn as a check? _____

Fill out the withdrawal slip. You want to withdraw $60 in cash from your account. It is account number 322221C.

FIRST FEDERAL SAVINGS
AND LOAN ASSOCIATION

WITHDRAWAL SLIP

I hereby apply for the withdrawal from my account in accordance with the charter of FIRST FEDERAL SAVINGS AND LOAN ASSOCIATION and I hereby acknowledge having received from said Association the below stated sum which the Association is hereby authorized to charge as a withdrawal against my account.

ACCOUNT NUMBER	AMOUNT WITHDRAWN	DATE

☐ Cash Withdrawal

☐ Check Withdrawal Payable to: _____

☐ Transfer to Account # (s) _____

_____
(signature)

_____
(address)

For Office Use Only

Check # _____

Approved by: _____

Writing Checks

When you have money in your checking account, you can write checks. A personal check is a form that tells the bank to pay money from your account to a person or a company. People use checks to pay bills (for example, utility bills or loan payments) or to pay for goods or services (for example, groceries or dry cleaning). A check is a safe way to send money through the mail.

When you open a checking account, you will order checks. The bank will give you a few checks to use until your check order arrives. The checks you order are bound together in a **checkbook.**

Do not write a check for more money than you have in your account! If your account is **overdrawn,** you do not have enough money in your account to pay a check you have written. The bank will say you have **insufficient funds.** You will pay a fee for each check that cannot be paid. The unpaid checks are called bounced or returned checks. A check may also be returned to you unpaid if you have not signed it or you have not filled it out completely.

The following descriptions will help you write checks. Fill in these six spaces on every check:

- Date: Write the month, day, and year. You may abbreviate. For example, *August 21, 2007* can be written as *Aug. 21, 2007, 8/21/2007,* or *8/21/07.*

- Pay to the order of: Clearly write the name of the person or company you are paying. This person is sometimes called the **payee.** Follow any directions that come with bills. Some bills tell you how to write the company's name.

- Amount in numbers: Write the check amount in numbers in the box after the dollar sign. Begin on the left side of the box. Use a decimal point to make dollars and cents clear.

- Amount in words: Write the same dollar amount in words on the long line that ends with the word *DOLLARS.* Write the cents as a fraction (for example, twenty-nine/100 or 29/100 to represent 29 cents). Begin on the left and try to fill the whole line. Draw a line through any extra space. This is to make sure no one can change or add to the number.

- Signature: Sign your check on the line at the bottom right. Do not sign a check until you are ready to mail it or give it to someone.

- Memo: Add information, such as an account number. Or write a note to remind yourself what the payment is for.

If you make a mistake on a check, you must **void** it. This means the check cannot be cashed. Write the word *VOID,* in large letters, across the check, and then tear it up. Keep track of voided check numbers.

REVIEW & PRACTICE

Look at the following sample check. Can you find all of the check features listed above?

Carlos Vallejos
101 Green St.
Dayton, Ohio 45415

0325

Date _May 15, 2006_

Pay to the
order of _Ohio Water Authority_ $ | 57.43 |

fifty-seven and 43/100 —————————— Dollars

ABC BANK & TRUST

Memo _4/06 water bill_   _Samuel Felicia_

|:098765432:000001111111:0325

Write a check to pay a phone bill. The phone company is General Telephone Company. Your phone bill is $68.70. Write the check for your phone payment. Fill in your name and address on the check.

_____

_____

_____ _____ 20 ____   204

Pay to the
order of _____ $ | |

_____ Dollars

FIRST FEDERAL SAVINGS
AND LOAN ASSOCIATION
NEW YORK, NY

Note: _____ _____

|:123456789:2200001111122:0000

Postal Money Order

One safe way to transfer money to another person is with a postal **money order.** A money order works like a check, but you do not need a bank account. Go to a U.S. post office and ask for a money order. Tell the clerk the amount in U.S. dollars and cents. Give the clerk that amount of money in cash. You will pay a small service charge for the money order.

Fill out the bottom of the money order. Write the name and address of the payee under *Pay to.* Write your name and address under *From.* On the top of the money order, write in the same *Pay to* information. Each money order has a serial number for identification. The number, the date, and the amount of the money order are on your receipt. Read the information and warning on the back. Carefully tear off the top part (customer's receipt) and keep it for your records.

The person who cashes a money order or a check has to show ID to the bank teller. Only the payee can cash a check or money order. That's why they are safe ways to send money through the mail.

REVIEW

Study the front and back of this money order. Then answer the questions.

CUSTOMER'S RECEIPT		
KEEP THIS RECEIPT FOR YOUR RECORDS	PAY TO, Yun Hyeok ADDRESS 6173 Park St., Chicago, IL 60626 C.O.D. NO. OR USED FOR birthday gift	SEE BACK OF THIS RECEIPT FOR IMPORTANT CLAIM INFORMATION **NOT NEGOTIABLE**

SERIAL NUMBER	YEAR, MONTH, DAY	POST OFFICE	AMOUNT	CLERK
06845264954	2006-06-26	132141	$50.00	004

POSTAL MONEY ORDER

SERIAL NUMBER	YEAR, MONTH, DAY	POST OFFICE	U.S. DOLLARS AND CENTS
06845264954	2006-06-26	132141	**$$$50∗00¢**

AMOUNT   FIFTY DOLLARS & 00¢∗∗∗∗∗∗∗∗∗∗∗∗∗∗∗∗∗∗∗∗∗∗∗∗∗∗∗∗∗∗∗∗∗

PAY TO Yun Hyeok	NEGOTIABLE ONLY IN THE U.S. AND POSSESSIONS SEE REVERSE WARNING
ADDRESS 6173 Park St.	FROM Yun Min
Chicago, IL 60626	ADDRESS 13 Lee Terrace, #4
C.O.D. NO. OR USED FOR Happy Birthday!	Marietta, GA 30006

I:000008002:   06845264954

1. What is the amount of the money order? _____

2. Is the same information on the top and bottom? _____

3. What instructions are on the receipt? _____

4. What is the reason for this money order? _____

KEEPING TRACK OF YOUR MONEY

Checking Account Register

When you open a checking account, you will receive a **check register.** A check register is a form you use to keep track of your account activity: deposits, withdrawals, and checks written on your account. It has lines for you to record your transactions.

Some checks have duplicates, or copies, behind them. When you write out a check, you keep the copy. But you should still fill out a check register to keep track of all the activity on your account.

A checking account register has columns for the transaction type or check number, date, description of the transaction, payment, or **debit** (amount of the check or withdrawal to be subtracted), and deposit, or **credit** (amount to be added). There may also be a column for fees. On the right, there is a column for your **balance** (total amount of money in the account after the transaction). Every time you make a transaction, write it in your register. Then add or subtract the amount in the balance column so you will always know how much money is in your account.

If you void a check, write that in your register. Write the check number and date, and write *void* in the transaction column. This keeps your check numbers in order to help you keep track of all of your checks.

Get a list of fees and service charges from your bank. Banks can subtract money from your account to pay fees. For example, there is a fee for every returned check. You need to subtract these fees from your account balance.

Some banks offer you access to your account records on the Internet. You can use a computer to pay bills online and to fill out an online account register. You can ask about online banking when you open your account.

Every month, the bank will send you a **statement**, or account activity summary. The statement lists every account transaction for the month. Use it to check your records. When you compare the bank statement to your check register, it's called *balancing your checkbook*. Instructions for balancing your checkbook are sometimes printed on the back of your statement. If you need help balancing your checkbook, call your bank.

With your statement, the bank may send photocopies of your **canceled checks.** These are checks you have written that have been paid. Keep these copies in case you need to prove that you have made a payment.

REVIEW & PRACTICE

Study the following checking account register.

TRANS / CHECK #	DATE	DESCRIPTION OF TRANSACTION	PAYMENT / DEBIT (–)	√	DEPOSIT / CREDIT (+)	$ BALANCE
						948.63
324	5/12	Grocery-Mart	79.81			79.81
						868.82
325	5/15	Ohio Water Auth.	57.43			57.43
		4/06 water bill				811.39
326	5/15	TMT Bank	364.95			364.95
		car loan				446.44
——	5/18	Paycheck			1171.15	1171.15
						1617.59
——	5/19	Cash withdrawal—	120			120.00
		ATM				1497.59
——	5/20	Service charge	4.00			4.00
		April				1493.59

1. When was the last withdrawal made? _____

2. What type of transaction was it? _____

3. How much is the monthly service charge for this account? _____

4. How much money was deposited during the month? _____

5. How many checks were written? _____

6. When was the last check written? What is the check number?

   _____

7. What is the total balance in the account now? _____

Practice filling in this checking account record. Begin with $300.86 in your checking account two weeks ago. Write the date. Enter a cash withdrawal five days ago for $50, a deposit (from your employer) for $175.10 yesterday, and check number 439 for $28.52, paid to your telephone company today. Add and subtract your transactions. What is your balance?

TRANS / CHECK #	DATE	DESCRIPTION OF TRANSACTION	PAYMENT / DEBIT (–)	√	DEPOSIT / CREDIT (+)	$ BALANCE

Savings Account Record

When you open a savings account, the bank will give you a savings account record. It will look similar to a checking account record. Use the record to keep track of your deposits and withdrawals.

If your checking and savings accounts are linked, you may get one statement for both accounts. If you have a separate savings account, you will receive a savings account statement, or activity record. Compare the statement to your savings account record to be sure your balance is correct.

REVIEW & DISCUSS

Answer these questions. Talk to your classmates about your experiences.

1. Who gets a joint bank account? Who gets an individual account?

2. What is interest on a bank account?

3. How do you open an account?

4. How do you deposit money?

5. What is direct deposit?

6. How do you withdraw money?

7. When do you need to endorse a check? How do you endorse it?

8. Why do you put lines after the amount when you write a check?

9. What is a PIN?

10. Why is a postal money order a good way to send money?

11. Have you used a U.S. postal money order? Explain the process to your classmates.

12. Does your bank have an ATM? A drive-up window? Explain your bank's services to your classmates. Share any experiences you have had using any of those services.

Consumer Concerns

KEY WORDS

consumer

donation

tax-deductible

purchase

warranty

upgrade

recall

refund

defective

exchange

credit

loan

annual fee

interest rate

grace period

installment plan

lease

deposit

Forms:

- mail offers
- catalog order form
- warranty/registration
- merchandise return form
- customer survey

- credit card application
- pre-approved credit application
- loan application
- rental agreement
- lease application

MAIL OFFERS

Consumers are people that use and buy products and services. Offers of products or services may come to you by mail, by phone, or online. A smart consumer carefully evaluates offers. Always study the good and bad points of an offer before you make a decision.

Sometimes people refer to unwanted mail offers as junk mail or spam. Junk mail is mail you do not ask for or want. Computer e-mail ads you do not ask for or want are called spam.

Offers for products or services can also be found in product packaging, in magazines, and in stores. The offers can be very tempting. The forms are often on postcards. They are quick and easy to fill out and send in. By sending in a postcard, you can get a free sample of a new product or a trial subscription to a magazine.

The following examples will help you read mail offers and give you practice with mail-in forms.

REVIEW

Read the following three mail offers. Answer the questions. Then fill out the offer cards. For more practice, bring in mail offers you have received at home. Show them to your classmates.

Yes! Start my trial subscription to **Love to Run** magazine. I agree to pay only $9.97 for the first year and receive 12 issues plus a free special issue, 13 issues in all! My check is enclosed.

Ms./Mrs./Mr. (circle one) _____ (Please print name)

ADDRESS _____ APT. NO. _____

CITY _____ STATE _____ ZIP _____

Money-back offer: satisfaction guaranteed, or we'll refund your money.

---

1. What kind of magazine is it? _____

2. Is there a guarantee? _____

3. What happens if you do not like the magazine? _____
_____

Electronic Supply Company, Inc. of Los Angeles

Special Bargain Prices on Electronic Equipment!

Sign up for our mailing list today and never miss another bargain for cameras, video and audio equipment, and computers. Low regular prices and frequent specials for preferred customers. Just fill out and send in the form below.

Yes! Send me your catalog and lists of bargains!

Name: _____

Address: _____
_____

E-mail: _____

---

1. What will you receive if you send in this card? _____
_____

2. Does Electronic Supply sell brand-name products? _____

3. Why do you think the card asks for your e-mail address?
_____

Around the Globe Organization

Thousands of people have helped protect wild animals worldwide for over 50 years. Won't you please help? Your $10 donation today will help create nature reserves for wild animals. Please give more if you can. Fill out the enclosed form and send us your check today.

Yes! I want to help save wild animals. My check for

_____ $10 _____ $25 _____ $50 _____ Other (fill in amount) is enclosed.

Name: _____

Address: _____

_____

For more information about **Around the Globe Organization** and its work, see the enclosed material or call our toll-free number: 1-888-555-ATGO.

Donations are tax-deductible.

Sometimes mail from an organization asks for a **donation**, or a gift of money. Read the information on the card.

1. What are the organization's goals? _____

2. Have you heard of the organization? _____

3. Is your donation **tax-deductible?** (Can you deduct or subtract the amount from your income taxes?) _____

Read mail offers carefully before you decide whether to respond. If you return the form, you may receive ads and offers from other companies as well. Keep track of any offers you reply to. And, if you make a donation, keep a record for your taxes.

CATALOG ORDERS

Catalog Order Form

Sometimes you use an order form to **purchase**, or buy, something from a catalog. You can order catalog items by phone, by mail, at a catalog center in a store, or over the Internet.

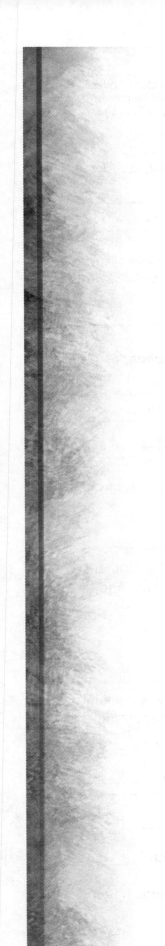

REVIEW & PRACTICE

Read the following catalog order form. What kind of information does the customer give?

Socks & Shoes
We have everything for your feet!

PO Box 000   Norcross, GA 30010
www.socks&shoes.foot   1-888-555-0000

Name **Connie Ede**   E-mail Address **conede@abc.mail**

Address **7581 Desert Rd.**   Daytime Telephone **520-555-4840**

City/State/Zip **Tucson, AZ 85718**

CATALOG #	SIZE	COLOR	DESCRIPTION	QTY.	PRICE	SUBTOTAL
P6300	7N	navy	Serena Pump, 2" heel	1	58.85	58.85
S0423	——	asst.	Knee highs, pkg. of 3	2	4.95	9.90
W7834	12EEE	black	Men's walking shoes	1	77.85	77.85

* Georgia residents must pay sales tax.

METHOD OF PAYMENT:

❑ Check or money order payable to **Socks & Shoes**

☒ VISA   ❑ MasterCard   Expiration date **03/09**

Card No. **9999-1234-9876-0000**

Signature **Connie M. Ede**

Order Date **7/25/06**

Merch. Total	146.60
Shipping	15.00
Subtotal	161.60
Sales Tax *	——
TOTAL	161.60

SHIPPING METHOD—Check method you prefer for continental U.S.

	❑ Ground	☒ 2nd day
up to $25	$5.00	$10.00
$25.01–50	$8.00	$12.00
$50.01–75	$9.00	$13.00
$75.01–100	$10.00	$14.00
$100+	$12.00	$15.00

For more practice, bring in a catalog with an order form. Fill out the form.

Online Order Forms

Many companies sell their products or services on the Internet. You can order books, music, clothing, and many other products that way. Be sure that the company has a privacy policy and security system for keeping your payment information private. A good company will tell you how it protects your information.

Most companies that sell items on the Internet have order forms that you can fill out and send electronically, by computer. These forms often require you to pay with a credit card.

PRODUCT WARRANTIES

When you buy some products, you may get a product **warranty** or registration card. New cars, appliances, and electronic equipment have warranties. When a company offers a warranty, it guarantees to repair or replace the product if there is something wrong with it. Some warranties have a time limit, for example, one year from the date of purchase. Warranties may also limit the types of problems covered.

The product warranty form gives the company useful information. Often it is a small mail-in card. Sometimes you can fill out the warranty information on the company's web site. The company will put your name and your purchase information in its records. Keep the registration card with your purchase receipt.

REVIEW

Look at the following mail-in warranty card. Then answer the questions.

PRODUCT WARRANTY REGISTRATION CARD

VWX 35mm Compact Camera

This camera is warranted against defective materials or workmanship for one year from the date of original purchase.

PLEASE PRINT

Name: _____

Address: _____

City: _____ State: _____ Zip: _____

Company: _____

E-mail: _____

Store where purchased: _____

Address: _____

State: _____ Zip: _____

Date of Purchase: _____ Model: _____ Serial No.: _____

---

1. Does the warranty cover defective parts? _____

2. Do you need to know where you bought the camera? _____

3. Why is it important to know the date the camera was purchased?

_____

AFTER A PURCHASE

Product Upgrades and Recalls

Sometimes a company offers buyers an **upgrade** (a newer version or added part) for a product. If your name is in the company's files, you may receive an upgrade notice. Upgrades are common for computer equipment and software.

A company may also **recall** (ask you to return) a product you own. For example, it may send a recall notice if a product is found to be unsafe. The company may offer to replace the product or **refund** (give back) your money. You may need to mail the product back to the company or return the product to a store. It is helpful to have the registration card and purchase receipt.

Customer Complaint or Return Form

Sometimes you are not happy with a purchase. A product may be **defective** (damaged or not working properly). You need to return it and get a refund. Sometimes you do not like the product. You might want to **exchange** it (take it back and get something else). Sometimes you want to discontinue or stop a service. You will need to fill out forms to solve these problems.

REVIEW & PRACTICE

Read the following return form and answer the questions.

For Trouble-Free Customer Service
- Complete this form and return in the enclosed envelope or with your returned book.
- This form is given priority processing. We apologize for your inconvenience.

Please adjust my account as follows:
☐ Correct my address as I have indicated below
☒ I am returning the following book(s):   Book code XY8743
                                             Book code _____

Please take the following action:
☒ Credit my account   ☐ Replace with Book code _____

Reason for return: ☒ Damaged   ☐ Wrong book on invoice
☐ The book received was not ordered   ☐ Other (explain below)
☐ I have this question, problem, or comment:

☐ Please write me.   ☐ Please call me at my daytime telephone: (___) _____

---

1. What did the customer order? _____

2. Why did the customer return the item? _____

3. What does the customer ask the company to do? _____

_____

Imagine that you bought a sweater from a catalog. It cost $30. The sweater is the right size, but you don't like the color (green). The color doesn't look like it did in the catalog picture. Use the customer form to ask for an exchange for a different color (red).

MERCHANDISE RETURN FORM

REASON CODES

Quality	**Size or fit**
11 Damaged or soiled	20 Too large, long, wide
12 Defective material or workmanship	21 Too small, short, narrow
14 Parts missing	
Color	**Service/handling**
30 Items not color matched	41 Order delayed/needed sooner
31 Color not as shown in catalog	51 Not as ordered/advertised

IMPORTANT: Please enter the most appropriate reason codes (see above).

Reason Codes	Qty. Rtn.	Reorder	Qty.	Catalog No.	Item	Color/ Size	Price	Tax

Name _____

Address _____

_____

_____

Phone _____

Check the appropriate box:

☐ Reorder

☐ Credit my account

☐ Cash refund

☐ Repair

Customer Opinion or Satisfaction Survey

Sometimes a company or store will ask your opinion. Restaurants often ask customers if they were satisfied with the food and service. There may be a form on the table or near the front door. Some consumer organizations send out forms with questions about many different products. If you purchase an item on the Internet, you may get an e-mail asking you to fill out a survey about your purchase experience.

Customer opinion surveys are optional. You do not have to fill out the forms or answer the questions. A customer survey should be anonymous. That means you do not need to sign your name. However, the company may promise to enter you in a prize drawing if you write your name.

Read the following customer survey. Practice filling out the survey.

Sally's Steakhouse
How would you rate us?

Please let us know how you feel about Sally's Steakhouse. We rely on your comments and suggestions to make Sally's your favorite choice for great food and dining.

Date _____   Time _____

Meal(s) ordered _____

1. Rate the following with 5 being the highest. Circle:
   Overall dining experience   1 2 3 4 5
   Food quality   1 2 3 4 5
   Hospitality   1 2 3 4 5
   Service   1 2 3 4 5
   Cleanliness   1 2 3 4 5

2. Was your dining experience a good value for the money? Yes _____ No _____

3. How did you hear about us?
   ❑ Phone book   ❑ Newspaper   ❑ Friends   ❑ Other _____

You can find customer surveys at restaurants, at stores, and on the Internet. Look for customer surveys when you go out to eat or to shop. Bring them to class for more practice.

CONSUMER CREDIT

When you use **credit,** you can purchase an item, take it home, and pay for it later. You can use a bank credit card or a store credit card. You charge a purchase on the card and a statement is sent to you later. The statement shows the total amount that you owe. You can make monthly payments or pay off the total amount.

You can use credit to pay for something slowly over a long period of time. In addition to credit cards, you may also apply for credit in the form of a **loan,** an installment plan, or a mortgage (for a house). You repay loans by making payments that include interest.

Careful consumers use credit to build a good credit record. They use credit carefully to buy things they can pay off quickly. A good credit record helps you get credit for major purchases like a house or a car.

Credit Cards

Using credit wisely shows that you can pay your bills and pay them on time. If you use a credit card to charge purchases, you will receive a bill later (usually in a few weeks). When you pay your bills regularly, you establish a good credit record.

Be careful when you choose a credit card. Some cards have high **annual fees.** This means the company will charge you money every year to use the card. Credit cards from different companies or banks have different **interest rates.** The interest is the amount you pay to charge your purchase. The bank will add interest to the amount you

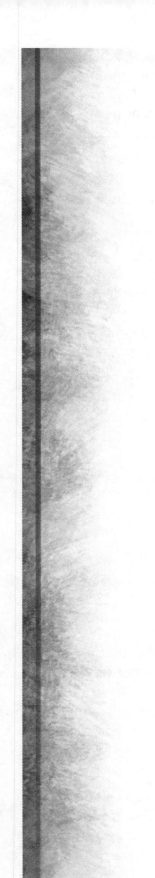

owe every month until you pay off the total amount. Shop around to get the best interest rate and lowest fees.

Many banks, companies, and organizations offer credit cards. Sometimes offers for credit cards come in the mail. When you consider a credit card offer, study the detailed information. Look at the **grace period** (number of days before your payment is due), interest rate, and other fees or penalties. Read the privacy statement and fine print. Choose and use credit cards carefully.

REVIEW & PRACTICE

Read this credit card application and answer the questions. Then fill out the application. For more practice, bring in a credit card offer that you have received in the mail. Talk about the offer with your classmates.

ABC Bank & Trust Copper Card
❑ **Yes, I want miles and more!**

You're pre-approved to earn dividend miles just for doing what you always do. Take advantage of this exclusive offer today and receive 7,000 bonus dividend miles the first time you use your card.

Simply complete and return the attached Copper Acceptance Certificate, or visit www.mycoppermiles.card. Do it today to get your free miles!

Copper Acceptance Certificate

Social Security Number	Home Phone
Birth Date	Employer/Business Name
Business Phone	Gross Yearly Household Income*
Mother's Maiden Name	E-Mail Address

* Income from alimony, child support, or separate maintenance payment need not be revealed if you do not wish us to consider it as a basis for repayment.

By signing below, you agree to the authorizations, terms, and conditions in the disclosure section.

Applicant Signature	Date
X	/ /

Authorized User (You request an additional card for the following person who is authorized to use your account.)

First Name	M.I.	Last Name

Fee and Term Information

Annual Percentage Rate (APR) for Purchases	Variable Purchase APR, currently 17.25% for Copper
Other APRs	Cash Advance APR: 19.5%. Default Rate: 22.75%
Variable Rate Information	Your APR for purchase, cash advance, and balance transfer transactions may vary. The rate is determined monthly by adding a margin to the Prime Rate: 10.0 for purchases and balance transfers and 13.0 for cash advances.
Balance Calculation Method for Purchases	Average Daily Balance (including new purchases)
Annual Fee	$95
Grace Period for Purchases	At least 20 days
Minimum Finance Charge for Purchases	$.50 (unless purchase Average Daily Balance is zero)

Late Charge: $30, Overlimit Fee: $30, Cash Advance Fee: 5% of each advance (min. $20). Total Foreign Currency Conversion Adjustment: 3% of foreign transaction. The information listed above is correct as of 11/1/06 and is subject to change at any time without prior notice.

1. What company is offering the card? _____

2. What is the annual fee? _____

3. What is the grace period? _____

4. What is the interest rate on a cash advance? _____

MAKING MAJOR PURCHASES

Long-term Loans and Installment Plans

When you make an expensive purchase—like a new car—you may want to pay for it over a long period of time, like five years or more. You can apply for a loan. A bank, credit union, or finance company will look at your credit record and decide if you qualify for a loan. Then you will make monthly loan payments that include interest.

Sometimes stores offer an **installment plan.** For example, if you buy new furniture, the store may offer to let you pay in installments or monthly payments. You promise in writing to pay off the total bill in a certain amount of time. Some installment plans do not add interest if you pay the full amount within a short period of time.

If you have good credit, you may receive mail offers for credit cards, car loans, and home loans or mortgages. Sometimes the offers are pre-approved. But you still have to fill out the application and send it in.

REVIEW & PRACTICE

Study the pre-approved credit application. Then fill out the loan application.

PRE-APPROVAL APPLICATION	FAX TO 888-555-1111 TO GET CREDIT TODAY!		NO APPLICATION REFUSED!	
CREDIT APPLIED FOR JOINT (INDIVIDUAL)	DEALER'S NAME Country Motors	BUYER'S DRIVER LICENSE NUMBER X023 8774 9999		STATE IL
NAME, LAST Kuti	FIRST Aisha	M. INITIAL A	DATE OF BIRTH 9/13/1987	APPLICANT'S PHONE 630-555-0708
ADDRESS 32 Winding Trail, Apt. # 4B		(MARRIED)	UNMARRIED	SEPARATED
CITY Cissna Park	STATE IL	ZIP 60924	SOCIAL SECURITY NUMBER 999-77-0021	MONTHLY TAKE-HOME $1760
BUYER'S EMPLOYER Cissna Hotel	ADDRESS/LOCATION Commerce Blvd., Cissna		PHONE 630-555-8888	HOW LONG
APPLICANT'S SIGNATURE Aisha A. Kuti	DATE 10/30/06	JOINT APPLICANT'S SIGNATURE		DATE

I attest that I am at least 18 years old and the information in this form is accurate and complete. I authorize the investigation of my credit and employment background and the release of any information about my credit history.

FIRST FEDERAL SAVINGS AND LOAN ASSOCIATION

PART I

CREDIT APPLICATION

DATE	AMOUNT REQUESTED	TERM	PAYMENT DATE DESIRED	PROCEEDS OF LOAN TO BE USED FOR

APPLICANT INSTRUCTIONS—PERSONAL
Part II Must Be Completely Filled-In Except for Shaded Area Which Is Optional

TITLE ☐ MS. ☐ MISS ☐ MR. ☐ MRS.	NAME LAST (Jr. or Sr.) FIRST		MIDDLE	NO. of DEP.	DATE OF BIRTH

ADDRESS NO. & STREET	CITY	COUNTY STATE	ZIP CODE	YEARS	SOCIAL SECURITY NO.

FORMER ADDRESS NO. & STREET	CITY	COUNTY STATE	ZIP CODE	YEARS	RESIDENCE PHONE

ARE YOU A U.S. CITIZEN? ☐ YES ☐ NO IF NO, DESCRIBE IMMIGRATION STATUS	DO NOT COMPLETE IF THIS APPLICATION IS FOR INDIVIDUAL UNSECURED CREDIT	☐ MARRIED ☐ SEPARATED ☐ UNMARRIED (INCL. SINGLE, DIVORCED, WIDOWED)

YOUR JOB	PRESENT EMPLOYER	POSITION	NO. YEARS THERE	WAGES $	☐ WEEKLY ☐ BI-WEEKLY ☐ MONTHLY

ADDRESS NO. & STREET	CITY	STATE	BUSINESS PHONE

FORMER EMPLOYER (IF LESS THAN 3 YEARS) ADDRESS

PART II

FINANCIAL CHECKING—BANK BRANCH	SAVINGS—BANK BRANCH

DEBTS—LIST ALL BANKS, STORES, LOAN & FINANCE COMPANIES, CREDIT UNIONS, AND OTHERS TO WHOM YOU ARE INDEBTED. INCLUDE ANY REVOLVING LINE OF CREDIT. USE EXTRA SHEET IF NECESSARY.

CREDITOR & ACCT. NO.	MONTHLY PAYMENT	PRESENT BALANCE
CREDITOR & ACCT. NO.	MONTHLY PAYMENT	PRESENT BALANCE
LANDLORD OR MORTGAGE HOLDER ☐ RENT ☐ OWN	MONTHLY PAYMENT	PRESENT BALANCE
AUTO—LIEN HOLDER	MONTHLY PAYMENT	PRESENT BALANCE

CREDIT REFERENCES	

ARE THERE ANY UNSATISFIED JUDGMENTS AGAINST YOU? ☐ YES ☐ NO
WERE YOU EVER BANKRUPT? ☐ YES ☐ NO OMIT IF MORE THAN 10 YEARS

CREDIT INQUIRIES

I authorize the Lender to make whatever credit inquiries it deems necessary in connection with this credit application or in the course of review or collection of any credit extended in reliance on this application. I authorize and instruct any person or consumer reporting agency to compile and furnish to the Lender any information it may have or obtain in response to such credit inquiries and agree that same shall remain your property whether or not credit is extended. All information set forth in this application is declared to be a true representation of facts for the purpose of obtaining the credit requested and any willful misrepresentation on this application could result in criminal action.

APPLICANT'S SIGNATURE	DATE

FOR BANK INFORMATION ONLY:	
Driver's License	Other ID

Rental Agreements

You need a good credit record to **lease** (borrow) a car, furniture, or an apartment. Your credit record is the history of how you use credit and pay bills. The rental company or apartment manager will ask you for personal and financial information to check your credit history.

Often you need to pay a **deposit.** A deposit is money you pay ahead of time, as a promise. Later you may get the money back or be able to use it toward a purchase. Read any rental or lease agreement carefully. When you sign it, you agree to the conditions in the contract.

REVIEW & PRACTICE

Read the following online order form. Then fill out the Renter Information section. Then fill out the lease application.

RFU   RENT-FROM-US

> **FLEXIBLE PAYMENTS:** At RFU, you choose what you want to rent and how you want to pay: weekly, bimonthly, or monthly.

> **TRY IT, THEN BUY IT:** At RFU, you can rent what you want without any long-term obligation.

> **90 DAYS = CASH:** All your rental payments from the first 90 days can be applied toward purchase.

> **OUR GUARANTEE:** We guarantee you will be happy within the first week or we will give you your money back.

ONLINE ORDER

STEP 1—RENTER INFORMATION

First Name [   ]   Last Name [   ]

Birth Date [   ]   Sex ○ Male   ○ Female

Social Security # [   ]   E-mail [   ]

Address [   ]   Apt. # [   ]

City [   ]   State [   ]   Zip [   ]

How long have you lived at this address? [   ]

Landlord/Mortgage Co. [   ]   Phone [   ]

Monthly Payment Amount [   ]   Move-in Date [   ]

Lease/Mortgage in whose name? [   ]

Length of Lease/Mortgage [   ]

Utilities in whose name? [   ]

Phone [   ]   Type [   ]

Other # [   ]   Type [   ]

Some items I'm interested in renting are:

☐ TV   ☐ Widescreen TV   ☐ Stereo
☐ Computer   ☐ DVD   ☐ Living Room
☐ Air Conditioner   ☐ Bedroom   ☐ Washer/Dryer
☐ Refrigerator   ☐ Dinette   ☐ Other

Parkside Apartments Lease Application

Date: _____ Apartment Number: _____

Applicant's Name: _____ S.S. Number: _____

Birthdate: _____ Sex: _____ Driver's License #: _____ State: _____

Spouse's Name: _____ S.S. Number: _____

Birthdate: _____ Sex: _____ Driver's License #: _____ State: _____

Present Address: _____ City: _____ State: _____ Zip: _____

Phone #: _____ Renting: _____ Move-In Date: _____ Move-Out Date: _____

Monthly Rental Amount: _____ Name of Landlord: _____

Landlord Phone Number: _____ Reason for Leaving: _____

Previous Address: _____ City: _____ State: _____ Zip: _____

Move-In Date: _____ Move-Out Date: _____ Rented? _____ Monthly Rental $: _____

Name of Landlord: _____ Landlord's Phone Number: _____

Employment:

Current Employer's Name & Address: _____ Zip: _____

Phone #: _____ Date Started? _____ Take Home Pay: _____

Type of Work: _____

Previous Employer's Name & Address: _____ Zip: _____

Phone #: _____ Date Started? _____ To _____

Other Income: Source: _____ $ Per Month _____

Given name, date of birth, and relationship of all persons (other than yourself) who will occupy the apartment.

_____

Credit References: List all charge accounts, credit cards, and loans you have:

Name	Address	Balance Owed	Monthly Payment	Paid as Agreed (Yes or No)
_____	_____	_____	_____	_____
_____	_____	_____	_____	_____

Bank: _____ Address: _____ Type of Account: _____

In case of emergency, person who may have apartment key:

Phone #: _____ Address: _____

Relationship to you: _____

Applicant represents that all of the above statements are true and complete, and hereby authorizes verification of above information, references and credit records. Applicant agrees to the terms of the "Application Deposit Agreement" below.

Application Deposit Agreement

Applicant has deposited an "Application Deposit" (in the amount stated below). If applicant is approved and a lease is entered into, the Application Deposit shall be credited to the required damage deposit ($100). If applicant is approved but fails to enter into a lease, the Application Deposit shall be forfeited. The Application Deposit will be refunded only if applicant is not approved. Keys will be furnished only after lease and other rental documents have been properly executed by all parties and only after applicable rentals and damage deposits have been paid.

Application Deposit: $50

Applicant's signature _____ Spouse's signature _____

Leasing agent: _____ Date: _____

REVIEW & DISCUSS

Answer these questions. Talk to your classmates about your experiences.

1. Collect your mail offers for products and services for one week. Bring the offers to class. As a group, evaluate the offers. What are the good and bad points of each one? Which offers might be worthwhile? Which ones are junk mail?

2. Collect other consumer forms and bring them to class. For example, pick up a customer satisfaction survey or an apartment rental form. Compare and discuss the forms.

3. What is credit? How do you build a good credit record?

4. Do you have any credit cards or store charge cards? Tell your classmates how and when you use them.

5. As a group, make a list of ways to be a careful, smart consumer.

Education and Employment

KEY WORDS

residency requirement

discriminate

Equal Opportunity Employer (EOE)

benefit

salary

wage

employment history

references

W-4 form

withhold

human resources

terminated

unemployment insurance

Forms:

- course registration form
- job application
- W-4 form
- unemployment insurance application

GETTING AN EDUCATION

Education and employment opportunities go together. Some people may need education or training before they are ready to apply for a job. And some people continue to study while they are working and throughout their lifetimes.

Taking Classes

Every community has many places where you can go to take classes, learn new skills, or study a language. To find classes, check with a local high school or community college, an occupational training facility, or a community center near you.

To apply for a class, you will fill out a course registration form. Usually there is a fee. You will need to pay a deposit or sometimes the full amount when you apply. Use a check to pay by mail. Do not mail cash. Some schools accept credit card payments over the phone or online.

Sometimes you need to meet a **residency requirement** to be eligible for a class or program. This means you need to show proof that you live in a specific town or school district.

REVIEW & PRACTICE

Look at the following sample course listing and registration form. Answer the questions. Then fill out the blank registration form.

Local School District Community Classes for Adults

ESL Conversational English:
Improve your language skills. Work on interaction skills and personal speaking. All learning materials are supplied. Classes meet M + W, 7–9 pm, Sept. 10 – Dec. 12. Fee: $30 Town residents only; minimum age 16.

        E-1 ESL—beginning level   Town Hall Room 1A
        E-2 ESL—intermediate level   Town Hall Room 1B

CS1 Introductory Computer Skills:
Learn basic computer skills for home, school, or work. This course is intended for beginners with little computer experience. Class meets M, 7–9 pm, Sept. 10 – Dec. 10. Williams Elementary School Computer Lab. Fee: $40 Town residents; $60 all others.

LOCAL SCHOOL DISTRICT REGISTRATION FORM

Computer classes are open to non-residents on space-available basis. All other courses are for town residents only. Minimum age: 18. Registration refunded if class is canceled. Make check or money order payable to: District Community Classes. Bring or mail to High School District Office.

NAME: _Roberta DeFrancisco_

ADDRESS: _1500 Maple St._

CITY, STATE, ZIP: _Los Angeles, CA 90061_

PHONE (Home): _555-1234_   (Work): _555-6600_

Course # and Title	Location	Tuition
CS1 Intro. Computer Skills	Williams ES Comp Lab	$40

        Total: _$40_   √ check   ____ money order

Signature: _Roberta DeFrancisco_   Date: _8/22/06_

1. What course will this person take? When does it meet? Where?

    _____

2. How much does it cost? _____

3. Can a person take both an ESL class and the computer skills class? Why or why not? _____

4. Do you have to be a resident to take a computer class?

    _____

Use the following information to fill out the following form. Your local school district offers a class called "Job Search Strategies," course number 03-1001. The course meets on six Tuesday nights from 6–8 p.m., starting October 9. It meets in Room 210 of Wilson High School. The cost is $75.

COURSE REGISTRATION FORM

NAME: _____

ADDRESS: _____

CITY, STATE, ZIP: _____

PHONE (Home): _____ (Work): _____

Course # and Title	Location	Tuition
_____	_____	_____
_____	_____	_____

Total: _____ _____ check _____ money order

Signature: _____ Date: _____

GETTING A JOB

Filling Out a Job Application

To apply for a job, you will fill out a job application. You put information about yourself and your skills and experience on the form. Sometimes you complete the form at the workplace. Or you might pick up an application to fill out at home. Then you bring it or mail it to the workplace or office. Some employers have applications available on the Internet. You can use a computer to print an application or to apply online for a job.

It is important to fill out a job application carefully and correctly. It is also a good idea to keep a copy of your application. That way you know what information you have provided to the employer. That will help you prepare for a job interview.

Sometimes a job application asks for personal information (e.g., marital status, citizenship, health, etc.). This information may be optional. And an employer cannot **discriminate**, or treat you unfairly, because of your race, national origin, sex, age, religion, or disability. If the job has a minimum age requirement, it is OK for the employer to ask you for proof of your age.

In a job ad, *EOE* means **"Equal Opportunity Employer."** An EOE employer follows the federal law and does not discriminate when

hiring. All applicants will be considered equally if they meet the work requirements for the job.

Social Security Number

Before you get a job, you will need a Social Security number. Every person born in the U.S. can get a Social Security number at birth. Parents need their children's Social Security numbers in order to claim them as deductions on their annual income taxes. Everyone needs to have a Social Security number to attend school, to apply for government assistance, or to work in the U.S.

When you work, part of your pay goes into the Social Security system. Your pay record shows how much money goes to Social Security. When you retire, or if you become disabled and cannot work, you will get monthly payments from Social Security. The Social Security Administration keeps a record of the money you have put into the system and calculates your **benefit** (the amount you are able to receive).

If you do not have a Social Security number, you will need one. Contact your local U.S. Social Security office (or a U.S. consulate or embassy overseas) for a copy of the form and information. The application comes with instructions and it lists the documents you will need to provide in order to get a U.S. Social Security number.

You can get a Social Security card application online or at your local Social Security office. The web address for the application is listed in the Resources section at the end of this book. You can find contact information for the U.S. Social Security Administration in the government pages of your local phone book.

Before you fill out the form, read the instructions. Ask for help at your local Social Security office if you need it. The instructions can seem complicated. They also explain laws about information privacy. Read carefully as you fill out the form. Some questions are optional (for example, questions about race or ethnic group).

After you complete the form, you must submit it in person at the Social Security office and show your documents to a government official. After your application is approved, a Social Security card with your number on it will be sent to your mailing address.

REVIEW & PRACTICE

Read the following job application. Then answer the questions.

APPLICATION FOR EMPLOYMENT
Please print clearly.

Date:
March 8, 2007

Name (Last) Garcia	(First) Juan	(M) Manuel	Suffix (e.g., Jr.) ——

Address 100 S. Fourth St.	City Wagner	State PA	Zip Code (+4 optional) 17841

Area Code 570	Home Phone Number 555-4567	Social Security Number 999-888-0000	

Position: Head Cook, Grove Ave. Restaurant	Position Code: FS10

Salary or Wage Required $10–$12 per hour	Job Availability: Immediately	What kind of position are you applying for? _X_ Full time ___ Part time

How many hours can you work per week? Up to 60	U.S. Military Service: None

U.S. Citizen? _X_ yes ___ no   If no, do you have a valid work permit?

EDUCATION

Have you graduated from High School or received a High School equivalency diploma? _X_ Yes ___ No   If no, highest grade completed ___

SCHOOL	NAME	ADDRESS	DATES ATTENDED	CREDITS COMPLETED	TYPE OF DEGREE	COURSE OF STUDY	DID YOU GRADUATE?
HIGH SCHOOL	Wagner H.S.	Wagner, PA	1996-1999				Yes
TECHNICAL OR BUSINESS	Centerville Occupational Skills Center	Centerville, NY	1999-2001	Culinary skills program	Completed two-year certificate program		Yes
COLLEGE OR UNIVERSITY	Centerville Community College	Centerville, NY	2001-2002			computer skills (online course); business; kitchen management	No
OTHER TRAINING	Wagner School District Adult Program: Advanced Conversational English, summer 1999 Advanced Culinary Workshops (weekends, summer 2004) Centerville Occ. Skills Ctr.						

Personal Information:

Community Activities Youth Soccer Referee, Wagner Team; Volunteer Parent: Boy Scout Troop 160, Wagner	Hobbies and Interests biking

Job-related Preferences: Indicate yes or no for each, plus any explanations

Are you willing to travel? No	Are you willing to relocate? No	Are you willing to work nights? Yes (until midnight)	Do you have a driver's license? Yes

Other Information:

General Health:
Excellent

Do you speak a language other than English fluently? Yes	If yes, which language(s)? Spanish

Computer Skills? (If yes, please explain)
Yes. I have training in word processing and basic spreadsheets.

Have you ever been convicted of a crime? ___ Yes _X_ No   If yes, explain.

EMPLOYMENT HISTORY

EMPLOYER	SUPERVISOR AND TITLE	MAY WE CONTACT?	From:	To:
Main Street Café	William O'Malley, Manager	yes	Jan. 2004	present
Address: 500 S. Main St. Wagner, PA	**Phone:** 570-555-8200	**Job Title:** Assistant Cook	Full Time	

Description of job duties:	Reason for leaving:
responsible for helping prepare breakfast, lunch, and dinner in family-style restaurant; responsible for fresh produce selection and salad preparation; sometimes assist the baker in dessert preparation	ready to have more responsibility in a restaurant kitchen

EMPLOYER	SUPERVISOR AND TITLE	MAY WE CONTACT?	From:	To:
Centerville Diner	John Wilson, Manager	yes	1999	2003
Address: 2120 E. Valiant Drive Centerville, NY	**Phone:** 518-555-9900	**Job Title:** Kitchen Assistant	Began as intern, then part time, became full time in 2002-2003 until I moved back to Wagner	

Description of job duties:	Reason for leaving:
Duties ranged from dishwashing and occasionally helping to clear tables to working with the kitchen staff (chef, short-order cook, baker, etc.) as needed. Had more responsibilities when I was hired full time.	I moved back to Wagner to assist a family member.

REFERENCES
List at least two people, in addition to previous employers, who can be contacted as references:

1. Mrs. Johanna Graber Culinary Skills Instructor Centerville Occupational Skills Center 5000 Apple Grove Parkway, Centerville, NY Ph. 518-555-0400	2. Antonio Garza Scoutmaster, Boy Scout Troop 160, Home address: 3002 Grant Blvd., Wagner, PA Ph. (home): 570-555-8765

Applicant Statement

CERTIFICATION: I certify that the statements made by me on this application are true and complete to the best of my knowledge and are made in good faith. I understand that if I knowingly make any misstatement of fact, I am subject to disqualification and dismissal and to such other penalties as may be prescribed by law or personnel regulations. All statements made on this application, including employment information, are subject to verification as a condition of employment.

SIGNED: *Juan Manuel Garcia*   DATE: March 8, 2007

1. What job is the person applying for? Does it have a job code?

   _____

2. What is the desired salary? _____

3. Is the applicant a U.S. citizen? _____

4. What date is he willing to begin the job? _____

5. What education or training does he have that relates to the job?

   _____

6. Does he include information that shows his leadership skills? If so, what? _____

7. Does he indicate any job preferences? If so, what are they?

_____

8. Do you think he is qualified for this job? Why or why not?

_____

Parts of a Job Application

The following descriptions will help you to fill out job applications. Look back at the completed application to see what these parts may look like.

- Personal information: Write your name, address, and contact information.

- Social Security number: Write the nine-digit number in three groups. Sometimes this is abbreviated: _Soc. Sec. No., SSN,_ or SS#.

- Position desired: Write the title of the job. If the employer uses a code number for a specific position, write that too.

- **Salary** or **wage:** This is the amount of pay you expect for the position. The pay depends on the kind of job it is and how much experience you have. If you are not sure what to write, leave this line blank. You can discuss it with the employer during your interview.

- Date ready to start: This is the date you can begin work. Be honest. If you want to complete a training course first, give a start date after your course ends. If you already have a job, you may need to tell your present employer you are leaving two to four weeks before you go.

- Sometimes you may need to write an end date. That is the last day you can work in that job. (For example, if you are a student applying for a summer job, give an end date before the next school semester starts.)

- Education: Write your education history. Start with your most recent schooling or classes. List vocational training programs, higher education, high school, etc. Include training courses in job skills. If English is not your first language, include recent ESL classes.

- Community activities: These are activities outside work or school. List activities that will tell the employer about skills you may have, like leadership or business skills.

- Organization membership: Some examples are trade unions, sports teams, school-parent organizations, etc. You do not need to list organizations that show your race, national origin, or religion.

- Hobbies or interests: List active things you like to do in your free time, such as playing a musical instrument, hiking, stamp collecting, etc.

- Availability: Write the days and hours you are willing to work. Think about times you cannot work or prefer not to work. The application may also ask if you are willing to work late hours. If the job has night shifts (work times at night) and you cannot or do not want to work at night, write *no*.

- Travel: Some jobs require travel, sometimes far from your home. If you are willing to travel for the job, write *yes*.

- Relocate: Some jobs may require you to move to a different city. Tell whether you are willing to move to the job location.

- Health: A job application may ask about your general health and physical ability to do the job. For some positions, you may need to pass a physical exam.

- Employment history: This is a list of your past jobs. Begin with your current or last job, and then list the job before that, and so on. Write the contact information for each employer.

- **References:** You may be asked for a list of references. These are people the employer may call to ask questions about you. References should be people who know you well but are not related to you, such as a teacher, coach, or former supervisor. Ask people if it is OK before you use them as references. Most applications ask for names and contact information for two or three references.

- Contact current employer: Some forms ask if it is OK for the company to contact your current employer. If you do not want your current employer to know you are looking for another job, you can say *no*.

- Signature: When you sign the application, you promise that everything you have written is true. Sometimes there is a statement above your signature. Read it carefully before you sign. By signing the form, you give the employer permission to verify or check the information you have provided.

PRACTICE

Fill out a job application. Use the completed form as a model. If you are applying for a job, bring the application form to class. Or, go to a local store or company and ask for an application.

WHEN YOU GET A JOB

Working people in the U.S. must pay taxes. When you begin a job, your employer will ask you to complete a **W-4 form.** A W-4 is a government form that tells your employer how much money to **withhold** (keep out of your paycheck) for federal taxes.

On the form, you add up your personal *allowances*. You get one allowance for yourself and one for each child or dependent. The allowances are used to figure out how much is withheld from your check for taxes. You will file a new W-4 form if your situation changes, for example, if you have a child.

Someone from your employer's **human resources** or personnel office can help you fill out your W-4. The top of the form and the second page (not shown here) give details about the allowances for different family income levels. The form also includes a worksheet.

The W-4 form is a U.S. government form. You must provide accurate information and sign and date the form. You submit the bottom of the page to your employer. Keep the top part for your records.

REVIEW & PRACTICE

Read the W-4 form, and then answer the questions.

┄┄┄┄┄┄ **Cut here and give Form W-4 to your employer. Keep the top part for your records.** ┄┄┄┄┄┄

Form **W-4**	**Employee's Withholding Allowance Certificate**	OMB No. 1545-0074
Department of the Treasury Internal Revenue Service	▶ **Whether you are entitled to claim a certain number of allowances or exemption from withholding is subject to review by the IRS. Your employer may be required to send a copy of this form to the IRS.**	20**06**

1 Type or print your first name and middle initial. _Carl N._	Last name _Burry_	2 Your social security number _000:99:0000_

Home address (number and street or rural route)
302 James Ave

3 ☐ Single ☒ Married ☐ Married, but withhold at higher Single rate.
Note. If married, but legally separated, or spouse is a nonresident alien, check the "Single" box.

City or town, state, and ZIP code
New York   NY 10001

4 If your last name differs from that shown on your social security card, check here. You must call 1-800-772-1213 for a new card. ▶ ☐

5 Total number of allowances you are claiming (from line **H** above **or** from the applicable worksheet on page 2) **5** _4_

6 Additional amount, if any, you want withheld from each paycheck **6** $ _20_

7 I claim exemption from withholding for 2006, and I certify that I meet **both** of the following conditions for exemption.
• Last year I had a right to a refund of **all** federal income tax withheld because I had **no** tax liability **and**
• This year I expect a refund of **all** federal income tax withheld because I expect to have **no** tax liability.
If you meet both conditions, write "Exempt" here . . . . ▶ **7**

Under penalties of perjury, . . . e best of my knowledge and belief, it is true, correct, and complete.
Employee's signature
(Form is not valid unless you sign it.) ▶ _Carl N. Burry_   Date ▶ _9/18/06_

8 Employer's name ar . . . ending to the IRS.)	9 Office code (optional)	10 Employer identification number (EIN)

---

1. What is the total number of allowances this person claims? _____

2. What additional amount does he want to have withheld? _____

3. If you filled out this form, how many allowances would you claim? _____

IF YOU LOSE A JOB

If your employment is **terminated** or ended (you lose your job), you may be eligible for state **unemployment insurance** benefits. To find out if you qualify, you fill out an unemployment application telling about the job. If you qualify for unemployment benefits, the state will send you benefit payments. Unemployment benefits can help support you and your family while you look for a new job. Usually you receive benefits for up to six months.

Each state has different procedures and forms. Go to your local unemployment office to apply for unemployment insurance. Some states allow you to fill out the form online. Or you can print the form, fill it out, and mail or bring it to the unemployment office. Some states ask you to check in regularly by phone or by computer to prove that you are actively looking for a job. In general, unemployment insurance forms are very long (5–8 pages). If you need help filling out the form, go to your local unemployment office. The following sample form includes key sections found on most state forms.

REVIEW & PRACTICE

Read the following unemployment insurance form. Notice the information it requests. Then answer the questions.

UNEMPLOYMENT INSURANCE APPLICATION

1. Social Security Number:	

2. Last Name:	First Name:		MI:

3. Address: Number and Street	Apt. No.	P.O. Box
City State	Zip Code	County

4. (Area Code) Phone Number:	

5. Birth Date:	Month	Day	Year

6. Gender:	☐ Male ☐ Female
7. Citizenship (check one):	☐ I am a U.S. citizen. ☐ I am a Permanent Resident of the U.S.
8. Are you a Military Veteran?	☐ No ☐ Yes
9. Ethnic Heritage (check one):	☐ Hispanic or Latino ☐ Not Hispanic or Latino ☐ I choose not to answer
10. Race (check one):	☐ White ☐ Native Hawaiian or Pacific Islander ☐ Black or African American ☐ Asian ☐ American Indian or Alaskan Native ☐ Other ☐ I choose not to answer
11. Education: Highest Grade or Degree Completed:	
12. Do you have a disability?	☐ No ☐ Yes ☐ I choose not to answer
13. Did your employer tell you that you would be returning to work within the next 45 days?	☐ No ☐ Yes
14. Are you seasonally unemployed and expect to be recalled within the next 6 months?	☐ No ☐ Yes

15. List the following:
   a) Name(s) of all employers you worked for in the last 18 months.
   b) Period of employment.
   c) Wages earned for each employer in the last 18 months.
   d) How were you paid (specify hourly, weekly, monthly, annually, commission, or at a piece rate)?

a) Employer Name	b) Dates Worked From: ___/___/___ To: ___/___/___	c) Earnings $ _____	d) How Paid _____
b) Employer Name	b) Dates Worked From: ___/___/___ To: ___/___/___	c) Earnings $ _____	d) How Paid _____

16. Why are you no longer working for your very last employer? (Lack of work includes temporary layoff or on-call status.)	☐ Laid off, lack of work, on-call ☐ Fired ☐ Quit ☐ Strike or lockout ☐ Still working part-time

Briefly explain in your own words the reason you are no longer working for your very last employer, within the space provided. Please do not include any attachments.

Reason: _____

_____

I hereby authorize all employers for whom I worked, health care providers, insurance carriers, pension administrators, the Social Security Administration, and schools to release information needed to process my application. All of my statements on this application are true.

Your application cannot be processed if you check No.   ☐ No   ☐ Yes

SIGN HERE _____   TODAY'S DATE: _____

1. Do you have to answer questions 9 and 10? _____

2. Why do you think questions 13 and 14 are on this form?

   _____

3. What information is required about your previous employer?

   _____

4. Do you have to tell about a job you had 3 years ago?

   _____

5. Do you have to tell why you are no longer working? _____

REVIEW & DISCUSS

Answer these questions. Talk to your classmates about your experiences.

1. Where can you go in your local area to take job training or career development classes?

2. What kinds of courses are available? (If possible, bring in some sample class lists and descriptions.) Are there classes for personal development (sports, art, etc.)?

3. What education and work skills do you need for the job you have or the job you want?

4. What is Social Security?

5. When do you need to fill out a W-4 form?

6. What is withholding?

7. What is a personal allowance? Give an example.

8. Who may apply for unemployment insurance benefits?

9. What information do you have to provide on an unemployment insurance application form?

10. Describe your present job and how you got it.

Health Care

KEY WORDS

primary care physician (PCP)

medical history

health insurance

health maintenance organization (HMO)

allergies

immunizations

wellness

urgent care

premium

co-payments

enroll

exclusion

claim

out-of-pocket expenses

Forms:

- medical history
- patient billing and insurance information form
- medical insurance enrollment form
- government health care form

FILLING OUT A MEDICAL HISTORY FORM

The doctor that coordinates your health care is called your **primary care physician (PCP).** You visit your PCP for regular checkups and for treatment of medical problems. Your PCP also refers you to specialists when necessary. The doctor's office will collect and keep your medical records and personal **medical history.** Your medical history is a list of all your major health problems and operations. It includes any serious health issues you and your immediate family members have had.

If you do not have a PCP, talk to friends, family members, or co-workers to find a doctor. If you have **health insurance** (insurance that helps pay your medical expenses), you may need to choose a doctor who is covered by your insurance company. Check with the insurance company or the doctor to be sure you are covered.

Call the doctor's office and make an appointment. Say that you are a new patient. Some offices are part of **health maintenance organizations (HMOs).** In an HMO, a group of doctors work together in one medical office. You may be able to make an appointment with any available doctor.

Your new doctor will need your medical history. Many offices mail you the form to fill out before your appointment. Sometimes it is called a health history or a patient health summary. The form has a lot of questions about your past and present health.

A personal health history form will ask about major illnesses (times you were very sick) or major injuries (times you were seriously hurt). You also need to list times you were in the hospital and any operations or surgeries you have had. The form may also ask about **allergies** (serious physical reactions to certain things like foods or medications), childhood diseases, and **immunizations** (shots to protect you from diseases).

You may need to list information about the health of your immediate family members. This includes your parents, your brothers and sisters, and any children you have. Knowing the health history of your close family members helps the doctor understand your health.

The information on your health history form is only for your doctor and other health care providers. It is confidential, or private, information. You must give your permission in writing for anyone else to read or have access to your medical history. Keep a copy of your medical history for your own records.

Medical history forms use a lot of medical vocabulary. Ask for help at the doctor's office if there are unfamiliar words on your doctor's form.

REVIEW & PRACTICE

Read the following medical history form and answer the questions. Then fill out the blank medical history form with your own information. If you do not want to share certain medical information with your teacher or classmates, leave the section blank. When you fill out your doctor's form, be sure to fill in every section.

Northside Medical Center
PATIENT MEDICAL INFORMATION FORM

Today's Date: __May 14, 2006__

Patient's Name: __William Chung__   Date of Birth: __2/24/1974__

Overall health (check one) ☐ Excellent   ☒ Good   ☐ Fair   ☐ Poor

Personal Health History

Check any of the following major health conditions or diseases that you have had or now have:

Medical Conditions:
- ☐ Asthma or breathing problems   ☐ Diabetes
- ☒ High blood pressure   ☐ Heart condition (be specific) _____

Childhood Diseases: ☒ Chicken pox   ☐ Mumps   ☒ Measles   ☐ Diphtheria

Hospitalizations or Operations: (include one-day surgeries as well as other hospital stays). Women: you do not need to include normal delivery of a baby in this list. Include any unusual conditions related to giving birth.

Hospitalization date (or your age then)	Reason (be specific)
Age 14	appendix removed

List any allergies you have (foods, insect bites, etc.). Be as specific as possible.

__Allergic to peanuts, strong reaction to bee stings__

List any major injuries. Give the year and type of injury.

__1982 broke my left arm__

List any prescriptions you are presently taking.

Name of medication	Dosage (amount and frequency)
None	

List any non-prescription medications you take regularly (vitamin supplement, pain reliever, etc.).

Name of medication	Amount and frequency
Multivitamin	one tablet every day

Personal Health Questions

Check yes or no. If yes, please explain.

Do you have any eyesight problems?	☒ Yes	☐ No	I'm nearsighted; I wear glasses
Do you have any hearing problems?	☐ Yes	☒ No	
Do you have any joint pains?	☒ Yes	☐ No	occasional pain in left shoulder
Do you frequently get headaches?	☐ Yes	☒ No	
Have you ever smoked?	☒ Yes	☐ No	If yes, please answer the next three questions.

If yes, how much?   __One pack a day__

Do you still smoke?   ☐ Yes   ☒ No

If no, for how long did you smoke, and when did you quit?   __I smoked for 10 years but stopped two years ago__

Do you drink alcohol?   ☒ Yes   ☐ No

If yes, how much? __one can or glass of beer each week__

Do you drink tea or coffee? (caffeine)   ☒ Yes   ☐ No

If yes, explain. __one or two cups of coffee every morning and evening__

Do you follow any special diet?   ☐ Yes   ☒ No

If yes, please explain. _____

Do you exercise regularly?   ☒ Yes   ☐ No

If yes, please explain the type of exercise and frequency. __I swim three times a week, and walk whenever I can.__

Immunization Record

Indicate the year you last received the following immunizations or booster shots:

Diphtheria/Tetanus __1995__   Measles/Mumps/Rubella __1978__

Influenza (flu shot) __None__   Tuberculin test __2004__

Other _____

Family Health History

Age now—any major medical conditions. If deceased, age/reason for death.

Father __57 high blood pressure_____

Mother __55 None_____

Siblings __Sister 27-None, Brother 29-None, another sister-died age 3, accident___

Children __4, 6_____

Patient's occupation __checkout clerk__   Employer __City Office Supplies, Inc.__

Marital status   ☐ Single   ☒ Married   ☐ Separated   ☐ Divorced   ☐ Widowed

In case of emergency, contact:

Name of person _____Edith Chung_____   Relation to the patient ___spouse_____

Contact information: Day phone: __555-1213__   Evening: __same_____

Patient's signature: _William Chung_____   Today's date: __May 14, 2006__

Note to Patient: Please complete the separate patient billing and insurance information form.

1. How old is the patient? _____

2. What medical condition does he have? _____

3. Has he had any childhood diseases? If so, which ones? _____

   _____

4. Has he had any operations? _____

5. What allergies does he have? _____

6. Does he mention any major injuries? If so, which ones? _____

   _____

7. Does he take any prescriptions or non-prescription medications? If so, what? _____

8. Does he have eyesight or hearing problems? Explain. _____

   _____

9. Does he drink coffee? If so, how much? _____

10. Does he exercise regularly? _____

11. How many siblings (brothers and sisters) does he have? _____

12. Who does he list for an emergency contact? _____

Family Medicine Associates
PATIENT MEDICAL HISTORY

Today's Date: _____ /_____ /_____   Date of Birth: _____ /_____ /_____

Patient's Name: _____
                        Last   First   Middle

Birthplace: _____ Sex: _____

Allergies: ☐ NONE   ☐ Bee Sting   ☐ Meds: _____

               ☐ Foods: _____   ☐ Other: _____

Current Medications: ☐ NONE _____

_____

Current/Chronic Medical Conditions: ☐ NONE _____

_____

Past Medical Problems (year/age):   ☐ NONE _____

_____

Surgeries (year/age):   ☐ NONE _____

_____

Are you currently employed?   ☐ YES ☐ NO   Occupation _____

Marital Status: ☐ Single   ☐ Married   ☐ Separated/Divorced   ☐ Widowed

Tobacco Use: ☐ NONE   ☐ Current   ☐ Prior _____ yr started _____ yr quit

                       Amount/type: _____   # yrs. _____

Alcohol Use: Beer / Wine / Spirits   ☐ rarely   ☐ weekly   ☐ daily

                       # of drinks per day / week _____   Do you have a problem with alcohol? _____

Drug/Nutrient Supplement use:
List all non-prescription medications you take regularly (include vitamins, antacids, pain meds, minerals, etc.).

_____

_____

Diet/Exercise: Your current diet is: ☐ satisfactory ☐ unsatisfactory

                    Your current weight is: ☐ satisfactory ☐ unsatisfactory

                    Your current exercise level is: ☐ satisfactory ☐ unsatisfactory

Family Medical History: ☐ No knowledge of family medical history

Race/Ethnicity (optional): _____

Relation	Age	Health Status	If deceased, Cause/Age at death
Father			
Mother			
Siblings			
Children			

Please indicate all conditions which apply to members of your family (brother, sister, father, mother, aunt, uncle, grandparent) and note relationship or additional concerns below:

☐ asthma/allergies   ☐ headaches   ☐ gallbladder
☐ arthritis   ☐ seizures/epilepsy   ☐ liver disease
☐ high blood pressure   ☐ stroke   ☐ kidney
☐ high cholesterol   ☐ thyroid disorder   ☐ breast disease (benign)
☐ diabetes   ☐ tuberculosis   ☐ breast disease (cancer)
☐ heart disease   ☐ chronic lung disease ☐ alcoholism/substance abuse
☐ bleeding/clotting disorder ☐ ulcers   ☐ mental illness

Patient's signature: _____   Today's date: _____

Patient Billing and Insurance Information Forms

When you go to a doctor's office, you will need to provide information about your medical insurance. The doctor needs to know who will pay your medical bills. Questions about medical billing may be part of your health history form or they may be on a separate form.

These descriptions will help you fill out billing and insurance information forms. A sample form is on the next page.

- Nearest relative not living with you: This is a close relative who lives in the same city or state. It can be an adult child, a parent, or a brother or sister.

- Referred by: Write the name of the friend, relative, or doctor who gave you this doctor's name.

- Guarantor: This is the adult who guarantees or promises to pay the bills. If the patient is a child, the guarantor is usually a parent or guardian.

- Insurance information: Write the name of the insurance company and your insurance identification number. If you have health insurance, you have an insurance card that lists this information. Your doctor's office will ask to make a copy of your card.

- Authorization and release statement: This is your permission to give medical information to the insurance company. When you sign it, you give permission to the doctor to release that information. The statement also authorizes the insurance company to pay the doctor.

REVIEW & PRACTICE

Read the following patient billing and insurance information form. Then answer the questions.

PATIENT INFORMATION

PLEASE PRINT

DATE: 01/10/2006

First Name: Elise   Middle Initial: M   Last Name: Cordeau

Street: 320 Blackburn Street, Apartment 11-C

City: Loma Mar   State: CA   Zip: 94021

Home Phone: 805-555-0010   Work Phone: Ext:

Birth Date: 10/04/1999   Social Security #: 999-00-4321   Sex: F

Dependent Child ☒   Spouse ☐   Other ☐ (please specify)_____

Adult Patients Only—complete this section:

Marital Status: Single ☐   Married ☐   Divorced ☐   Separated ☐   Widowed ☐

Employer: Work Phone:

Spouse's Name: Work Phone:

All Patients:

Nearest relative not living with you: Jean Cordeau   Phone: 805-555-1189

Referred by: John Wagner, father of Karen Wagner, patient of Dr. Janson

IF THE PATIENT IS NOT RESPONSIBLE FOR THE BILL, PLEASE FILL IN THE FOLLOWING LINES

Guarantor's First Name: Pierre   Middle Initial: L   Last Name: Cordeau

Street: 320 Blackburn Street Apartment 11-C

City: Loma Mar   State: CA   Zip: 94021

Home Phone: 805-555-0010   Work Phone: 805-555-9845 Ext: 21

Birth Date: 03/27/1975   Social Security #: 999-00-6666   Sex: M

Relationship to Patient: Father

Employer: Brown Transport Company

INSURANCE INFORMATION

Primary Insurance Co. Name: CareSelect, Inc.

Subscriber's Name: Pierre Cordeau   Date of Birth: 03/27/75   Soc. Sec.: 999-00-6666

ID #: BTC 12345   Group #: 06000ZF

I understand and agree that regardless of my insurance status, I am ultimately responsible for the balance of my account for professional services rendered. I will notify you of any changes in the patient's health status or any changes in insurance status.

I hereby authorize the physician to provide my insurance company with all relevant medical information it may request. I further authorize my insurance company to pay the physician directly for services provided.

_____Pierre L. Cordeau_____   _____01/10/2006_____
Signature of patient or guarantor   Date

1. Who is the patient? Is she an adult or a child? _____

2. Who referred the patient or guarantor to this doctor? _____

3. What is the relationship between the guarantor and the patient?

   _____

4. Does the family have health insurance? _____

APPLYING FOR HEALTH INSURANCE

Health insurance can help protect you and your family from the high costs of medical care. A health insurance policy or plan often provides **wellness** (preventive care) benefits. These are routine services to help you stay healthy. Other benefits help you when you become sick or need **urgent care** (emergency medical care).

Many employers offer group health insurance for employees and their families. Usually the employer pays part of the cost of the insurance, and the employee pays the rest. Your cost is your **premium.** Your employer may subtract your premium from your paycheck.

An employee may pay for insurance to cover other family members like a spouse or children. Insurance plans vary depending on how many people are covered, what types of services are covered, and how much you pay. Your employer will give you information about health plans and benefits (services covered). Some plans cover visits to the dentist or eye doctor. Or you may buy separate insurance to cover those expenses. Read and understand your choices before you decide.

Many insurance plans require **co-payments.** When you visit the doctor or get a prescription, your health insurance pays most of the cost. The remaining part of the cost that you must pay is your co-payment.

After you have decided on a health insurance program that fits your needs, you will need to fill out an application. The application will **enroll** you in (make you a member of) the insurance plan. Your employer's human resources office will help you.

When you get health insurance, you will receive an insurance card for yourself and for other members of your family who are covered. The card lists your name, the insurance company name, your subscriber (ID) number, and your doctor's name. A plan from your employer is a group plan, and your card will have a group number. Your insurance card may also list co-payment amounts.

You will also receive a copy of your health insurance policy. Be sure you understand your plan and the benefits, **exclusions** (things that are not covered), and costs.

REVIEW & PRACTICE

Read the following sample enrollment form for CARESelect insurance and answer the questions. Then fill out the blank insurance enrollment form.

CARESelect, INC.
ENROLLMENT FORM

Check Reason for Enrollment Form:

- ☒ new subscriber
- ☐ terminate coverage
- ☐ change name
- ☐ add a family member
- ☐ terminate a family member
- ☐ change primary care physician
- ☐ change address
- ☐ COBRA

PLEASE TELL US ABOUT YOURSELF (PLEASE PRINT)

Social Security No. *(Employee):* 999-99-1108	Social Security No. *(Spouse):* 999-99-2665

Marital status:
- ☐ Single ☒ Married ☐ Separated
- ☐ Divorced ☐ Widowed

Employee Name: *First:* Vladimir *MI:* N *Last:* Rusinoff

Employer: **Auburn Electric Company**

Home Address: 101 Main Street #9

Date of Employment: **2/7/06**

City: Auburn State: WA Zip: 98003

Type of coverage requested:
☐ Individual ☐ Two Person ☒ Family

Telephone: *Home:* 509-555-0400 *Work:* 509-555-9823

Requested effective date:
2	7	2006
Month	Day	Year

PLEASE GIVE US INFORMATION ON EACH PERSON TO BE COVERED

Important: You and each member of your family must select a Primary Care Physician from the Participating Physicians Directory. Dependent children must be under 19 unless a full-time student. For each full-time student, you must provide proof of enrollment to our Enrollment and Eligibility Department within 30 days of enrollment.

	LAST NAME FIRST MI	SEX	BIRTH DATE	PRIMARY CARE PHYSICIAN
1. Employee:	Rusinoff Vladimir N.	M	7/17/69	Dr. Walter Hanson
2. Spouse:	Rusinoff Anna R.	F	11/3/70	Dr. Lena Mattima
3. Child:	Rusinoff Peter A.	M	12/14/94	Dr. Judith Campion
4. Child:	Rusinoff Alexandra L.	F	2/28/92	Dr. Judith Campion

PLEASE ANSWER THE QUESTIONS BELOW

Have you or any member of your family ever been enrolled in CareSelect, Inc. before? ☐ Yes ☒ No	Will you or any member of your family be covered through another health insurance? ☐ Yes ☒ No
Is your spouse employed? ☒ Yes ☐ No	Are you transferring your coverage from any other carrier? ☐ Yes ☒ No

If yes, place of employment: **International Center, Bigville University**

PLEASE SIGN THIS ENROLLMENT FORM AND RETURN IT TO YOUR PERSONNEL OFFICE

1. On behalf of myself and any eligible dependents listed, I hereby apply for coverage under the CareSelect, Inc., contract issued by my employer.
2. I understand that except for life threatening emergencies, covered services must be obtained through a participating physician or participating hospital. I further understand that certain services may require prior approval from CareSelect, Inc. and/or a copayment by me or my dependents directly to the physician or hospital.
3. I hereby authorize any person or institution who provides services under this contract to make available to CareSelect, Inc., any medical information it requests, and understand that the information will be kept confidential.
4. I hereby represent to you that all information provided by me herein is true and complete to the best of my knowledge.

Employee's signature: *Vladimir N. Rusinoff* Date: 2/7/06

---

1. Is Mr. Rusinoff a new subscriber? _____

2. What type of coverage does he want? _____

3. How many dependents does he list? _____

4. Will this insurance cover dependent children over the age of 20?

_____

5. Do any family members have the same primary care physician?

_____

6. Has Mr. Rusinoff ever had CareSelect insurance before? _____

7. Does he have any other health insurance coverage? _____

8. What does Mr. Rusinoff's signature authorize? _____

_____

CARESelect, INC.
ENROLLMENT FORM

Check Reason for Enrollment Form:

☐ new subscriber   ☐ add a family member   ☐ change address
☐ terminate coverage   ☐ terminate a family member   ☐ COBRA
☐ change name   ☐ change primary care physician

PLEASE TELL US ABOUT YOURSELF (PLEASE PRINT)

Social Security No. *(Employee):*	Social Security No. *(Spouse):*	Marital status:
		☐ Single ☐ Married ☐ Separated ☐ Divorced ☐ Widowed

Employee Name: *First:*   *MI:*   *Last:*

Employer:

Home Address:

Date of Employment:

City: State: Zip:

Type of coverage requested:
☐ Individual ☐ Two Person ☐ Family

Telephone: *Home:*   *Work:*

Requested effective date:

Month   Day   Year

PLEASE GIVE US INFORMATION ON EACH PERSON TO BE COVERED

Important: You and each member of your family must select a Primary Care Physician from the Participating Physicians Directory. Dependent children must be under 19 unless a full-time student. For each full-time student, you must provide proof of enrollment to our Enrollment and Eligibility Department within 30 days of enrollment.

	LAST NAME FIRST MI	SEX	BIRTH DATE	PRIMARY CARE PHYSICIAN
1. Employee:				
2. Spouse:				
3. Child:				
4. Child:				

PLEASE ANSWER THE QUESTIONS BELOW

Have you or any member of your family ever been enrolled in CareSelect, Inc. before? ☐ Yes ☐ No	Will you or any member of your family be covered through another health insurance? ☐ Yes ☐ No
Is your spouse employed? ☐ Yes ☐ No	Are you transferring your coverage from any other carrier? ☐ Yes ☐ No

If yes, place of employment:

PLEASE SIGN THIS ENROLLMENT FORM AND RETURN IT TO YOUR PERSONNEL OFFICE

1. On behalf of myself and any eligible dependents listed, I hereby apply for coverage under the CareSelect, Inc. contract issued by my employer.
2. I understand that except for life threatening emergencies, covered services must be obtained through a participating physician or participating hospital. I further understand that certain services may require prior approval from CareSelect, Inc. and/or a copayment by me or my dependents directly to the physician or hospital.
3. I hereby authorize any person or institution who provides services under this contract to make available to CareSelect, Inc. any medical information it requests, and understand that the information will be kept confidential.
4. I hereby represent to you that all information provided by me herein is true and complete to the best of my knowledge.

Employee's signature: _____   Date: _____

Government-Sponsored Health Care Programs

Some people join an employer-sponsored group health plan. Others may pay for individual health insurance. And some people cannot afford health insurance. There are some federal and state health care programs for people that cannot afford insurance. You must meet certain requirements (for instance, family size or maximum income requirements) to be eligible.

Many government health program forms are long. They include the application and detailed instructions. There may also be a section called For Office Use Only. A government officer evaluates your application and decides if you are eligible for the program.

If you have to fill out a complex government insurance form, ask for help. Someone in your local branch of the government office, for example, a state social services office, should be able to help you. That person can answer your questions and explain anything you do not understand.

The National Health Information Center provides information about government health care programs. The web address for the center is listed in the Resources section at the end of this book.

PRACTICE

Read this enrollment form for the Family StayWell State Health Program. Then fill it out. Ask your teacher for help if you need it.

Family StayWell State Health Program

Please READ the entire application and INSTRUCTIONS before you fill it out.
Print clearly in blue or black ink. If you need more room for any section, attach an additional page.

Section A Contact Information Please tell us who you are and how to contact you.

First Name	Middle Initial	Last Name

Please give us a number where you can be reached if we need to contact you for more information.	Phone #	Another Phone #	Primary Language Spoken

HOME ADDRESS of the person(s) applying for health insurance.

Street	Apt. #

City	State	Zip Code	County

MAILING ADDRESS, if different.

Street	Apt. #

City	State	Zip Code	County

Section B Household Information List the names of everyone applying for health insurance and the names of their parents, stepparents, or spouses living with them, if they are not also applying. List the head of household on line 1.

First, Middle Initial, Last	Date of Birth	Sex M/F	Is this person a parent of any applying child? (Yes or No)	Is this person pregnant? (Yes or No)	Relationship to Head of Household	Does this person want health insurance? (Yes or No)	Social Security Number (applicants only)
Maiden name, if any:			❑ Yes ❑ No	❑ Yes ❑ No		❑ Yes ❑ No	
Maiden name, if any:			❑ Yes ❑ No	❑ Yes ❑ No		❑ Yes ❑ No	
Maiden name, if any:			❑ Yes ❑ No	❑ Yes ❑ No		❑ Yes ❑ No	
Maiden name, if any:			❑ Yes ❑ No	❑ Yes ❑ No		❑ Yes ❑ No	
Maiden name, if any:			❑ Yes ❑ No	❑ Yes ❑ No		❑ Yes ❑ No	

Is anyone in the household a veteran? ❑ Yes ❑ No	If yes, Name:

Section C   Health Insurance You or your family may still be eligible even if you have other health insurance.

1. Is anyone in the household already covered by a state or federal health program?   ☐ Yes   ☐ No

If yes	Name		ID
	Name		ID

2. Does anyone who is applying already have other health insurance?   ☐ Yes   ☐ No

If yes	Name of policy holder		
	Insurance Co.	Group #	Monthly Cost $
	Person(s) covered	End date of coverage	

Section D   Citizenship This information is needed only for those people applying for health insurance. Almost all children are eligible for health insurance regardless of immigration status.

Is everyone who is applying a U.S. citizen?   If Yes, skip to Section E.   ☐ Yes   ☐ No

If No, please give the following information for anyone applying for health insurance who is not a U.S. citizen. Your answers to these questions will be kept completely confidential.

First Name	M.I.	Last Name	Does this person belong to any of the categories listed below? Check the appropriate box.	If either A or B, enter date when the person entered the U.S. (mm/dd/yy)
			☐ A ☐ B ☐ None	
			☐ A ☐ B ☐ None	

A: Check A if the person is under one of the following categories:
* Legal Permanent Resident (green card holder)
* Asylee   * Refugee   * Amerasian
* Cuban/Haitian Entrant   * Withholding of Deportation
* Parolee for at least one year   * Conditional Entrant
* Battered immigrants and/or children
* Native American born in Canada who is at least 50% Native American

B: Check B if the person is under one of the following categories:
* Order of Supervision   * Voluntary Departure
* Deferred Action Status   * Stay of Deportation
* Suspension of Deportation   * Parolee for less than one year
* Covered by an approved immediate relative petition
* Properly filed or granted application for adjustment of status
* Has lived continuously in the U.S. since before January 1, 1972.
* Living in the U.S. with the knowledge and permission or acquiescence of the USCIS and whose departure USCIS does not contemplate enforcing.

Section E   Household Income List the types of money and the amount received by anyone listed in Section B.

Types of Income	Name of Person	How much?	How often?
Earnings From Work: (Include wages, salaries, commissions, tips, overtime, self-employment)			

If no income, please explain (for example, living with friend or relative):

Do you have to pay for child care (or for care of a disabled adult) in order to work or go to school?   ☐ Yes   ☐ No

If yes	Name	How much?	How often?

Section F   Housing Expenses

These questions help us determine the best program for the applicant(s). Answering these questions is optional if this application is only for children under the age of 19.

Monthly housing payment	Type of heat	Is heat included in housing payment? ☐ Yes ☐ No

I have been told my rights and benefits if I am eligible for this program. I have read and understand the conditions for eligibility and enrollment. I certify under penalty of perjury that everything on this application is the truth as best I know.

Signature   Date

Health Insurance Claims

Your insurance company needs to know when you visit your doctor. Often your doctor's office files the forms for routine covered services. For example, most health insurance plans cover an annual physical or checkup and any laboratory tests. You will probably sign a form at the doctor's office saying that it is OK for your insurance company to pay the doctor.

When you have a medical problem, you or your doctor's office will file a **claim.** A claim is a form requesting that the insurance company pay for medical services. Sometimes it is a computer form. Sometimes it is a printed form. For example, if you are injured or sick, you might need to go to a hospital for treatment. The insurance company will cover or pay for services included in your insurance plan. It may cover some or all of the services. In addition to a co-payment, you may have to pay some part of the cost yourself. The costs you pay for are called **out-of-pocket expenses.** The amount of costs that are covered depends on your insurance plan.

Read medical insurance claim forms carefully. Be sure the information is accurate. Carry your insurance card with you when you visit your doctor. Make sure the insurance information (ID number, group plan number) is correct on the claim form. While you are in your doctor's office, ask for help if you do not understand something before you sign the claim form.

Remember, when you sign a claim form, you authorize your doctor to tell your insurance company about your health and the medical services you received.

REVIEW & DISCUSS

Answer these questions. Talk to your classmates about your experiences.

1. Who needs a personal health history record?

2. Why do you think a health history includes questions about childhood diseases like chicken pox?

3. Why do you think a health history includes questions about smoking, drinking, coffee and tea, and exercise?

4. Why do you think a health history includes questions about a person's family members?

5. Who needs health insurance? Do you have health insurance? If so, do you know what is covered? Do you know what is not covered? Do you know what to do in the case of a medical emergency?

Driving and Automobile Insurance

driver's license

learner's permit

non-driver
photo ID

Department of
Motor Vehicles
(DMV)

driver's manual

license plates

registration

title

vehicle
identification
number (VIN)

passenger

liability
insurance

deductible

witness

pedestrian

claimant

Forms:

- driver's license application
- vehicle registration application
- auto insurance claim form

DRIVING A CAR

You need a **driver's license** or **learner's permit** to drive a car. A learner's permit allows you to drive under limited conditions until you pass the test for your driver's license. You also need a license to drive a truck or operate a motorcycle. In some states, you need a license to operate or drive other motor vehicles. For example, you may need a license to drive a boat or a snowmobile.

Your license is an official photo ID. If you do not drive a car, you may still need a photo ID. You can get a **non-driver photo ID** card.

Each state in the U.S. has different rules and applications for getting a driver's license. You can apply in person at your local **Department of Motor Vehicles (DMV)** office. Many states have the forms and instructions on the Internet.

Application for Driver's License

This form has seven major parts. The following descriptions will help you to fill out a driver's license application. Look at the application on pages 76–77 to see what these parts may look like.

A. General applicant information: This application is used for many different purposes. You check the reasons (one or more) that you are applying.

- ❏ Learner Permit: to learn to drive
- ❏ ID Card: to get a new license or a non-driver ID card
- ❏ Renewal: to renew your existing license from this state
- ❏ Replacement: to replace a lost, stolen, or destroyed card
- ❏ Change: to change information on your existing license
- ❏ Out-of-state License Conversion: to convert (change) your license from one state to another

The first five of these items and your residential address will be printed on your driver's license, learner's permit, or ID card:

- Name: Write your last name, first name, and middle name.

- Date of Birth: Use two digits each for the month, day, and year. For example, May 8, 1989 would be 05/08/89.

- Sex: Check the correct box.

- Height: Write your height in feet and inches.

- Eye Color: Write the color of your eyes.

- Social Security Number (SSN): Write the number in the boxes. You must have a Social Security number to get a driver's license.

- Day Phone No.: This is optional; you do not have to provide it.

- Mailing Address: Write the address where you get your mail. You may use a PO Box here or a mailing address. The motor vehicles department will mail your license to that address.

- Permanent Address: This is where you live. If this is the same as your mailing address, you do not have to write it again. You need to provide a residential address to get a driver's license.

- Changes: Answer these questions if you already have a learner's permit or previous license in this state.

  ✓ Has your name changed? Check *yes* or *no*. If yes, print your former name (look at your license and copy it exactly).

  ✓ Has your mailing address changed? Check *yes* or *no*.

  ✓ Has the address where you live changed? Check *yes* or *no*.

  ✓ Other changes: List whatever information you are changing or correcting.

B. License and driver history: If you are applying for a non-driver photo ID, you do not need to complete this section. All permit and license applicants must answer these questions.

If you answer *yes* to any of these questions, you may need to explain or supply documentation.

- Do you have a valid (current) learner's permit or driver's license in this state? If yes, write the permit or license number, date, and type.

- Do you have a valid driver's license in another state or an international driver's license? If yes, fill in the information.

- Do you have any medical condition that may affect your ability to safely operate a motor vehicle? If yes, check the appropriate boxes. The official may ask you more questions or require medical documentation.

- Are you currently taking any medication that could affect your ability to safely operate a motor vehicle? If yes, give a short explanation. (For example, you might have a prescription that makes you sleepy.) A DMV official may request medical documentation.

- Have you had a driver's license or learner's permit suspended, revoked, or canceled, or a license application denied in this state or elsewhere? If yes, go on to the next question: Has your license or permit been restored or your application approved? This is a legal question. People who commit a crime or cause a serious accident may have their license taken away or revoked. If it is taken away temporarily (suspended), they may get it back after some time.

Other questions—answer only the questions that apply to you.

- Are you applying for a commercial driver's license? (For example, you need a commercial license to drive a big truck for your job.)

- Are you requesting a written test or road test waiver? (Are you asking not to take the tests?) If you have already passed the tests in another state, you may not need to retake them. Read the description to see if you are eligible for a waiver.

C. Parent/guardian consent: Each state has a minimum age (usually 15 or 16) for a learner's permit and a driver's license. A teenager needs adult permission or consent to get a learner's permit or license. A parent or legal guardian needs to sign the form. Leave this section blank if it does not apply to you.

D. Voter registration questions: In many states, people may register to vote when they complete a license application.

- If you are not a U.S. citizen, you cannot register to vote. Check *No*.

- If you are a U.S. citizen and want to register to vote, check *Yes*. Then fill out the voter registration section. (There is more information on voter registration in Unit 8 of this book.)

E. State organ and donor registry: This is optional. You do not have to check this box. Read the information and decide. The Tissue/ Organ Registry is a state list of names of possible donors. If you check *Yes*, you will receive other information about the program. Many states print this donor information on driver's licenses or non-driver ID cards.

F. Certification and signature: Read this carefully. Make sure you understand it before you sign. Remember, when you sign the application, you are promising that all of the information is true. Before you sign, reread the form and your answers. This is a legal document, and the state will keep the information on file. Sign your full name. Then print your name in the other box.

G. <u>Office use only</u>: Do not write anything in this part. A DMV official or examiner will fill it out. Some of the boxes refer to other steps in the application process. After you submit the form, you will complete other steps. You may need to take various tests and show documents to prove identity and age.

- Vision Exam: You will have a brief vision exam or eye test to get a new license or to renew your license. The official may indicate a restriction (limit) on driving. For example, many people must wear glasses or contacts when they drive.

- Photo: A photo of you will be taken at the DMV for your license or ID card.

- Documents: You need to prove your identity and date of birth to get a new license or ID card. Usually you need to show two or more forms of identification. For example, you might present a passport or birth certificate and a credit card or existing driver's license. Each state has different requirements. Learn the requirements for your state and bring the appropriate ID.

- Written Test: You will take a written test to get a new license. Get a copy of the state **driver's manual** (rules for driving in that state), and study it. Ask someone to help you study. The written test is usually multiple-choice or true-false questions based on the information in the manual.

- Road Test: You also need to take a road test (driving test). You must pass the written test before you take the road test. The DMV will schedule your road test.

PRACTICE

First, look at the driver's license application and read the instructions at the top. Then fill out each part. Notice that some parts are optional.

APPLICATION FOR DRIVER LICENSE OR NON-DRIVER ID CARD
PLEASE *PRINT* CLEARLY

I AM APPLYING FOR A *(check any that apply):*

☐ Learner Permit ☐ Driver License ☐ Non-Driver ID Card ☐ Renewal ☐ Replacement ☐ Change ☐ Conversion

A. GENERAL APPLICANT INFORMATION

LAST NAME	FIRST NAME	MIDDLE NAME

DATE OF BIRTH			SEX		HEIGHT		EYE COLOR	SOCIAL SECURITY NUMBER* (SSN)
Month	Day	Year	Male ☐	Female ☐	Feet	Inches		

DAY PHONE NO. (Optional)

Area Code

( )

* Authority to collect SSN is granted in the V&T law. This information will be used only for exchange with other jurisdictions, to assist in verification of identity and to invoke driver license sanctions pursuant to V&T law section 510 (4-e). Your number will not be given to the public or appear on any form or information request.

ADDRESS WHERE YOU GET YOUR MAIL–Include Street Number and Name, Rural Delivery and/or box number (If PO Box, also fill in "Address Where You Live" below)

	Apt. No.	City or Town	State	Zip Code	County

ADDRESS WHERE YOU LIVE IF DIFFERENT FROM MAILING ADDRESS–DO NOT GIVE PO BOX

	Apt. No.	City or Town	State	Zip Code	County

Has your name changed?
☐ Yes ☐ No

Has your mailing address changed?
☐ Yes ☐ No

Has the address where you live changed?
☐ Yes ☐ No

If "Yes," print your former name exactly as it appears on your present license or non-driver ID card.

OTHER CHANGE: What is the change and the reason for it (new license class, wrong date of birth, etc.)?

B. LICENSE AND DRIVER HISTORY Must be completed by all learner permit and license applicants.

1. Do you now have, or did you ever have: a learner permit for this state? ☐ Yes ☐ No a driver license for this state? ☐ Yes ☐ No

   If "Yes," enter the identification number as it appears on the license or non-driver ID card.

   ID NUMBER

2. Do you have a valid license from another state, or an international driver license? ☐ Yes ☐ No

   If "Yes," where was it issued? _____ *Date of Expiration* _____

   Type of License _____ *Driver License No.* _____

3. Do you have any medical condition that may affect your ability to safely operate a motor vehicle? ☐ Yes ☐ No

4. Are you currently taking any medication that could affect your ability to safely operate a motor vehicle? ☐ Yes ☐ No
   Note: If you answered "Yes" to question 3 or 4, additional documentation may be required.

5. Have you had a driver license, learner permit, or privilege to operate a motor vehicle suspended, revoked, or canceled, or an application for a license denied in this state or elsewhere? ☐ Yes ☐ No
   If "Yes," has your license, permit or privilege been restored, or your application approved? ☐ Yes ☐ No

COMMERCIAL DRIVER LICENSE APPLICANTS ONLY
If you are applying for a Commercial Driver License, do you certify that you comply with all requirements? ☐ Yes ☐ No

ROAD TEST AND WRITTEN TEST WAIVER

If you have a license from another state or Canada, check the box to request exemption from the road test and written test.

☐ **I request that the road test and written test be waived because I have a license issued by another state or Canadian province that is valid, or that expired in the past year.**

By signing below, I certify that, when it was issued, I was a permanent resident of the state or province in which the license was issued, that I have been licensed for AT LEAST 6 MONTHS, and that I have not failed the road test for a driver license in the past 12 months. I understand that waiver of the road test and written test is at the discretion of the Commissioner of Motor Vehicles.

C. PARENT/GUARDIAN CONSENT

☐ Junior License

☐ Non-driver ID Card (under 16)

I am the parent or guardian of the applicant, and I consent to the issuance of a learner permit, license or (if under 16) a non-driver ID card to him/her. Note to parent/guardian: If the driver license applicant is 17 years old and has Driver Education Student Certificate of Completion, consent is not required.

Parent or Guardian
Sign Here →

(Relationship to Applicant)   (Date)

D. VOTER REGISTRATION QUESTIONS (Please answer "yes" or "no.")

If you are not registered to vote where you live now, would you like to apply to register, or if you are changing your address, would you like the Board of Elections to be notified?

NOTE: If you do not check either box, you will be considered to have decided not to register to vote.

☐ YES—Complete Voter Registration Application Section
☐ NO—I Decline to Register/Already Registered/I do not want to notify the Board of Elections of my change of address.

E. STATE ORGAN AND TISSUE DONOR REGISTRY

☐ The State Health Department has established a Registry for organ/tissue donors. By checking this box, you are authorizing the Department of Motor Vehicles to send your name to the State Health Department for inclusion in the Registry. The State Health Department will then send you more information about this lifesaving program.

F. CERTIFICATION

I state that the information I have given on this application is true to the best of my knowledge. If I am applying for a replacement license, I certify that I am the holder of a valid State driver license that is not now suspended or revoked, and that this license has been lost, mutilated or destroyed. If I am applying for a replacement non-driver ID card, I certify that I am the holder of a valid State non-driver ID card and that this non-driver ID card has been lost, mutilated, or destroyed. If the lost license or non-driver ID card is found after I receive the replacement license or non-driver ID card, I will turn in the original to the Department of Motor Vehicles. If I am using a credit card for payment of any fees in connection with this application, I understand that my signature below also authorizes use of my credit card.

SIGN HERE →
(Sign name in full)

PLEASE PRINT NAME

IMPORTANT: Making a false statement in any license or non-driver ID card application, or in any proof or statement in connection with it, or deceiving or substituting, or causing another person to deceive or substitute in connection with such application, is a misdemeanor under the Vehicle and Traffic Law, and may result in the revocation or suspension of your license or non-driver ID card.

G. OFFICE USE ONLY

PROOF:
☐ Passport

☐ Birth Certificate
☐ Learner Permit

☐ Driver License/ID
☐ USCIS Papers

☐ Credit Card
☐ MV-45

☐ Other: _____

TEST RESULTS:			Comments	Examiner's Initials
Eye	☐ Pass	☐ Corrective Lens		
Written	☐ Pass	☐ Fail		
Road	☐ Pass	☐ Fail ☐ Reject		

Special Restrictions as listed:

REGISTERING A VEHICLE

When you buy a new or used car, you need to register it (tell the state DMV about the car). When you register the car at the DMV, you will get **license plates** and a temporary **registration** sticker. The license plates and registration identify you and your vehicle. Your permanent registration will come in the mail. You need a **title** (proof of ownership) to register a car. You will get the title when you buy the car.

PRACTICE

Read the following form and fill it out. Use information about your own car or use this example. You just bought a used, 2004, 4-door, blue Toyota Corolla with a 4-cylinder gasoline engine. The car has a 6-number odometer. It has 46,252 miles on it. The **vehicle identification number (VIN)** is Z8A234567. The car weighs 2,597 pounds.

State Department of Motor Vehicles
VEHICLE REGISTRATION/TITLE APPLICATION
INSTRUCTIONS ⟶ COMPLETE BOXES 1–5. PLEASE PRINT CLEARLY.

❶ WHAT DO YOU WANT TO DO?

☐ REGISTER this vehicle for the first time   ☐ TRANSFER Plate Number _____ to this vehicle   ☐ CHANGE a title

☐ RENEW plate # _____   ☐ CHANGE registration for Plate Number _____   ☐ TITLE ONLY for a 1973 or newer vehicle

☐ REPLACE lost registration items   ☐ LEASE BUY-OUT Plate Number _____

❷

CLIENT ID NO. *(from Driver License of first registrant listed below)*

NAME CHANGE?   ☐ YES   ☐ NO

ADDRESS CHANGE?   ☐ YES   ☐ NO

Is this registration for a corporation or partnership?   ☐ YES   ☐ NO

NAME OF REGISTRANT *(Last, First, Middle)*

How was the vehicle obtained? ☐ New   ☐ Leased New   ☐ Used   ☐ Leased Used

DATE OF BIRTH

Month	Day	Year

SEX   M ☐   F ☐

DAY PHONE NO. *(Optional)*   Area Code ( )

ADDRESS WHERE YOU GET YOUR MAIL *(Include Street number and Name, Rural Delivery, and/or box number)*

	Apt. No.	City or Town	State	Zip Code	County

ADDRESS WHERE YOU LIVE *(IF DIFFERENT FROM MAILING ADDRESS—DO NOT GIVE PO BOX)*

	Apt. No.	City or Town	State	Zip Code	County

❸

VEHICLE IDENTIFICATION NUMBER

VEHICLE DESCRIPTION

Year	Make

Body Type For Cars

☐ 2-Door   ☐ 4-Door   ☐ Convertible

☐ Station Wagon/Suburban   ☐ Other _____

Body Type For Other Vehicles

☐ Pick-up   ☐ Van   ☐ Motorcycle   ☐ Tow

☐ Truck   ☐ Trailer   ☐ Other _____

Color

Unladen Weight

Type of Power (Fuel)

☐ Gas   ☐ Diesel   ☐ Electric   ☐ Propane

☐ Other ____

Cylinders	*For trailers & commercial vehicles* Max. Gross Weight	*For rentals, buses & taxis* Seating Cap.	Odometer Reading in Miles	Vehicle's ODOMETER has room for how many numbers (5, 6 or 7—do not include tenths)? ____	*For trailers & commercial vehicles* Axles / Distance

❹ ADDITIONAL VEHICLE INFORMATION ⟶ QUESTIONS 1-3 MUST BE COMPLETED.

1. I certify that, to the best of my knowledge, this vehicle ☐ has been or ☐ has not been wrecked, destroyed, or significantly damaged and rebuilt. (Checking the "has been" box means that the title issued will have the statement "Rebuilt" on it.)

2. Is this vehicle owned and registered by you for your own personal use?   ☐ Yes   ☐ No
   If "Yes," go to question 3 below. If "No," check any of the following boxes that apply:
   ☐ It is a passenger vehicle to be used for hire with a driver and operated as a taxi
   ☐ It is used only as a farm vehicle (Form MV-XX must be attached.)

3. Has this vehicle been modified to change its registration class?   ☐ Yes   ☐ No   If "Yes," explain _____

❺ CERTIFICATION The information I have given on this application is true to the best of my knowledge. I certify that the vehicle is fully equipped as required by the Vehicle and Traffic Law, and has passed the required State inspection within the past 12 months. I also certify that appropriate insurance coverage is in effect, and that the vehicle will be operated in accordance with the Vehicle and Traffic Law.

Print Name Here → _____
(Print Name in Full)

Sign Here → _____
(Sign Name in Full)

Additional Signature Sign Here → _____
(Sign Name in Full—Additional signature required if registering this vehicle in more than one name.)

INSURING A VEHICLE

When you register your car, you need to show proof that you have automobile insurance. The insurance protects you, your **passengers** or riders, and people in other cars if you are involved in an accident. To choose an insurance agency, ask for rate quotes (estimates for the cost of insurance) and compare them. You can get quotes from an insurance agent by phone, over the Internet, or at an insurance office.

The insurance company you choose will send you a bill for the premium. Auto insurance premiums may be paid monthly or once or twice a year. The insurance company will send you a copy of your insurance policy and a proof of insurance card to keep in your car.

Auto insurance coverage varies. Some states require a minimum amount of certain types. Ask an insurance agent about the requirements for your state.

Basic auto insurance is called **liability insurance.** If you cause an accident, you may be liable (responsible) for paying the costs. Liability insurance covers personal injury and property damage. States require different minimum amounts of personal injury and property damage insurance. Plus there are other types of coverage including collision and comprehensive insurance. Compare rates and ask questions to find out what you need.

Ask your insurance agent about the **deductible.** That is the amount you pay out-of-pocket before your insurance covers the rest of the costs.

IF YOU ARE IN AN ACCIDENT

If you are in an accident while driving, you need to report it to the police. You also need to tell your insurance company about the accident. You must report any accident that involves injury to a person or major damage to one or more vehicles.

Several forms must be filled out to report an accident. You should fill out a personal accident information sheet. The police fill out a report, and your insurance company will prepare an accident report and claim.

Accident Information Sheet

An accident information sheet is your personal record of an accident. It helps you write down and remember important details. The information sheet helps you give useful facts to the police and your insurance company. Sometimes an insurance company or an automobile association will give you an accident sheet to fill out. Keep a blank accident information sheet in your car with your insurance card.

Write the names, addresses, and phone numbers of any **witnesses** on your accident information sheet. A witness is someone who sees the accident. A witness may be a passenger in your car, someone in another car, or a nearby **pedestrian** (person walking).

PRACTICE

Imagine that while you were driving you were involved in an accident with another car. It was a sunny afternoon, about 2 p.m. You were coming to a stop sign at the intersection of Main Street and First Street and were getting ready to stop. The car behind you did not stop. It ran into the back of your car and damaged it. The front of the other car was dented. No one was hurt.

John S. Doe, manager of a nearby gas station, witnessed the accident and can describe what he saw. This form includes information about the other driver and car.

Complete the sample accident information form. Draw the cars to show their positions at the time of the accident. You are the insured. If you do not have a car, fill in an imaginary car and license number.

In a group, compare your forms. Are your drawings and descriptions of the accident similar?

VEHICLE ACCIDENT REPORT FORM

THIS FORM IS FOR YOUR PERSONAL USE TO HELP YOU IN THE EVENT OF A VEHICULAR ACCIDENT (AND AFTER) WHEN YOU MAY HAVE TO PROVIDE INFORMATION TO YOUR INSURANCE COMPANY AND YOUR STATE DEPARTMENT OF MOTOR VEHICLES.

Time _____ (A.M.) (P.M.)   Date _____

Place: **Draw** as best you can. Show where each car was at the time of the collision. If no other vehicle was involved, show where your car came to a stop. **Label** each street or road clearly. Indicate position of traffic lights, stop signs, etc. Indicate skid marks (if any), if you can. **Estimate** the speed of your car _____ mph, and of the other vehicle _____ mph at the time of the accident.

Show the direction of each car.

Road conditions: _____

Weather: _____

Name of other driver: _Thomas V. Scott_ _____

License # and state of other vehicle: _NY ZZZ0987_ _____

Vehicle—year, make, model, color: _1999 Dodge Caravan, red_ _____

Description of damage to other vehicle:

Description of accident:

Names of witness(es): _____

Address and Phone#: _____

Names of witness(es): _____

Address and Phone#: _____

If there is damage to property or injury to others, describe here:

Insurance Company Automobile Accident Report

Your insurance company will ask for information about an accident. Use your accident information form to answer questions. Someone from the insurance company will look at the damage to your car. You will need to take the car to a repair shop to get estimates for fixing the damage. Then the insurance company can decide how much it will pay for the repairs. The company will also want information about injuries or any other damaged property.

PRACTICE

Read this section of an accident report and insurance claim form. It asks for detailed information about an accident. Use the information from your personal accident information sheet. On the insurance form, you are the **claimant.** A claimant is a person filing an insurance claim form to get benefits.

Driving and Automobile Insurance **81**

VEHICLE ACCIDENT REPORT AND INSURANCE CLAIM FORM

CLAIMANT AND INCIDENT INFORMATION

CLAIMANT'S NAME (A separate form must be completed for each claimant.)	DATE OF ACCIDENT	TIME

CURRENT STREET (RESIDENCE) ADDRESS	CITY	STATE	ZIP	PHONE	HOME WORK

(RESIDENCE) STREET ADDRESS FOR SIX MONTHS PRIOR TO ACCIDENT	CITY	STATE	ZIP

CITY/STATE/COUNTY (if applicable) WHERE OCCURRED	STREET OR HWY.	MILEPOST NO.	INTERSECTION OR NEAREST STREET/ROAD

YOUR VEHICLE INFORMATION (VEHICLE #1)

YEAR	MAKE	MODEL	LICENSE PLATE NO.	WHERE CAN CAR BE SEEN?	WHEN?

NAME OF VEHICLE OWNER	ADDRESS	CITY	HOME AND WORK PHONE

NAME OF DRIVER	ADDRESS	CITY	HOME AND WORK PHONE

DRIVER'S LICENSE NUMBER	STATE OF ISSUANCE	DATE OF EXPIRATION

DESCRIBE DAMAGE	ESTIMATE $

OTHER NON-VEHICLE DAMAGE

WAS OTHER (NON-VEHICLE) PROPERTY DAMAGED? (If so, describe what type of property was damaged.)

NAME OF OWNER	ADDRESS	CITY	PHONE

DESCRIBE DAMAGE	ESTIMATE $

INJURED PARTIES

NAME	ADDRESS	PHONE	INJURY	AGE	VEH 1	VEH 2	VEH 3	PED	OTH
		HOME WORK							
		HOME WORK							

WITNESSES AND PERSONS WITH KNOWLEDGE OF LIABILITY OR DAMAGE FACTS

NAME (Attach additional sheets if necessary.)	ADDRESS	CITY	PHONE
			HOME WORK
			HOME WORK

COMPLETE ALL DETAILS

DATE OF ACCIDENT			TIME	LOCATION (STREET)	OR NEAR INTERSECTION OF:
MO	DAY	YEAR	☐ A.M. ☐ P.M.		

CITY AND STATE	TYPE:	☐ Front to rear	☐ Head-on	☐ Parked car	☐ Pedestrian
		☐ Broadside	☐ Sideswipe	☐ Bike-car	☐ Hit object

	#1 YOUR VEHICLE	#2 OTHER PARTY (NAME)	#3 OTHER PARTY (NAME)
1. If pedestrian, where was he/she (crosswalk, etc.)?			
2. At what distance was danger first noticed?			
3. Speeds at time danger was first noticed?			
4. Speeds at time of accident?			
5. What warning signals given?			
6. Obstruction to vision (weather and other)?			
7. Lights on? Wipers on? Windows fogged?			
8. Had any party been drinking? Who?			

REVIEW & DISCUSS

Answer these questions. Talk to your classmates about your experiences.

1. Who needs a driver's license?

2. What is a photo ID?

3. What is a learner's permit?

4. How do you apply for a driver's license in your state?

5. What documents do you need to show when you apply?

6. Does your state have an organ donor registry on the license application? What about voter registration?

7. How do you register a vehicle in your state?

8. Why is a sample accident information form important?

9. Are there times when it is not necessary to report an accident? Describe an accident that you would not report to the police or your insurance company.

10. Is the insured always the same as the operator?

11. Who can be a witness?

12. What kinds of information about an accident do you need for an accident report form for your auto insurance company?

13. Have you ever been involved in a car accident (as a driver, passenger, or witness)? Share your experiences.

Citizenship and Voting

KEY WORDS

customs declaration

prohibited

currency

resident

retail value

duty

naturalization

primary election

general election

affidavit

Forms:

- customs declaration
- naturalization application
- passport application
- voter registration

ENTERING THE U.S.

Everyone who enters the U.S. from another country must go through U.S. Customs & Border Protection (CBP). That includes U.S. citizens and citizens of other countries. You will fill out a **customs declaration** form when you arrive at the airport or port. The two-sided form asks questions about things you are bringing into the U.S. One person fills out the form for a family traveling together. Then you will show your customs declaration form and your passport to a CBP officer.

The following descriptions will help you fill out a customs declaration form. Look at the form on page 86 to see what the sections look like.

- **Family name:** Print your family name (last name) in the first white box. Then print your first (given) name and middle name.

- **Birth date:** Write the two-digit day, month, and year.

  Example: February 9, 1982 = Day ⬜9⬜ Month 0⬜2⬜ Year 8⬜2⬜.

- **Number of family members traveling with you:** Write the total number.

- **U.S. street address:** Write your address in the U.S. It may be your home address. A visitor can write the name and address of a hotel or the address of a relative's residence where they will stay.

- **Passport issued by:** Write the name of the country that issued your passport.

- **Passport number:** Copy this number carefully from your passport.

- **Country of residence:** Write the name of the country where you now live.

- **Countries visited on this trip:** List the names of the countries you have just visited.

- **Airline/flight no. or vessel name:** Write the name or the abbreviation for the airline name and the flight number. If you arrived by ship (vessel), write the ship name.

- **Primary purpose:** If this was a business trip, check *Yes*. If it was a vacation or pleasure trip, check *No*.
- **I am (We are) bringing:** This is a very important question, with four parts. Read and check each line. These are **prohibited** items. The items cannot be carried into the U.S.
- **I am (We have) been in close proximity of livestock:** Did you touch any livestock (farm animals such as cows or horses) on your trip? For example, if you worked on a farm and took care of livestock, you would check *Yes*.
- **I am (We are) carrying currency:** It is legal to bring up to $10,000 in U.S. **currency** (money) or the foreign equivalent. This question asks if you have more than that amount. If you do not, check *No*. Read the back of the form for more details.
- **I have (We have) commercial merchandise:** Did you bring any items you plan to sell? Most non-business travelers do not have commercial merchandise. If you have only personal items and souvenirs, check *No*.
- **Residents/Visitors—Total value of all goods and articles:** If you are a U.S. **resident** (a person who lives in the U.S.), fill in the first box. If you are a visitor (someone who does not live in the U.S.), fill in the second box.

PRACTICE

Fill out the customs declaration form on the next page. Follow the instructions on the form.

For practice, use the following information. You live in the U.S. You went to the Philippines to visit relatives. You did not go to a farm. You have U.S. $200 with you. You do not have any items for sale (commercial items). On your trip, you bought clothing ($165), a necklace ($45), and postcards and maps ($20). Your relatives gave you a gift. It is a traditional musical instrument (value $100).

U.S. Customs and Border Protection

Customs Declaration

19 CFR 122.27, 148.12, 148.13, 148.110,148.111, 1498; 31 CFR 5316

FORM APPROVED
OMB NO. 1651-0009

Each arriving traveler or responsible family member must provide the following information (only ONE written declaration per family is required):

1. Family **Name**

   First **(Given)**   Middle

2. **Birth date**   Day   Month   Year

3. Number of **Family members** traveling with you

4. (a) U.S. Street **Address** (hotel name/destination)

   (b) City   (c) State

5. **Passport issued by** (country)

6. **Passport number**

7. Country of **Residence**

8. **Countries visited** on this trip prior to U.S. arrival

9. **Airline/Flight No.** or **Vessel Name**

10. The primary purpose of this trip is **business**:   Yes   No

11. I am (We are) bringing

    (a) fruits, vegetables, plants, seeds, food, insects: Yes   No

    (b) meats, animals, animal/wildlife products: Yes   No

    (c) disease agents, cell cultures, snails: Yes   No

    (d) soil or have been on a farm/ranch/pasture: Yes   No

12. I have (We have) been in close proximity of (such as touching or handling) **livestock**:   Yes   No

13. I am (We are) carrying **currency or monetary instruments** over $10,000 U.S. or foreign equivalent: (see definition of monetary instruments on reverse)   Yes   No

14. I have (We have) **commercial merchandise**: (articles for sale, samples used for soliciting orders, or goods that are not considered personal effects)   Yes   No

15. Residents — the **total value of all goods,** including commercial merchandise I/we have purchased or acquired abroad, (including gifts for someone else, but not items mailed to the U.S.) and am/are bringing to the U.S. is: $

    Visitors — the **total value of all articles** that will remain in the U.S., including commercial merchandise is: $

Read the instructions on the back of this form. Space is provided to list all the items you must declare.

I HAVE READ THE IMPORTANT INFORMATION ON THE REVERSE SIDE OF THIS FORM AND HAVE MADE A TRUTHFUL DECLARATION.

X _____
  (Signature)   Date (day/month/year)

For Official Use Only

Read the Important Information on the back of the form. U.S. residents must declare all items acquired (bought or received) abroad. List them in the Description of Articles. You can put similar things in groups. For example, clothing could include T-shirts, a hat, and some baby clothes. List expensive items separately.

Write the **retail value** (cost in a store) for each item or group of items. Also list gifts from other people. Give the retail value of each gift. Add the values and write the total. Write that total in the box on the front of the declaration card.

Visitors must declare the value of items they will leave in the U.S. (for example, gifts for relatives). Write the total in the box on the front.

A Customs official reads the information and decides the **duty** (tax) you will pay. U.S. residents may bring items worth up to U.S. $800 without paying duty.

Reread your customs declaration form on both sides. Have you filled out the form correctly? Is everything true? Sign your name at the bottom of the front and write the date. Now you are ready to submit the form to a Customs officer.

BECOMING A U.S. CITIZEN

If you are born in the U.S., you are a U.S. citizen. You can also become a U.S. citizen by **naturalization.** A person who is born outside the U.S. and meets requirements for U.S. citizenship can become a naturalized citizen.

You must meet eligibility requirements to become a naturalized U.S. citizen. You must fill out the N-400 Application for Naturalization. The form is very long and has many parts. You give information about yourself and your family. You also give residence information, your employment record, and travel history (a list of the trips you have taken abroad). The form has detailed instructions on separate pages.

PRACTICE

Fill out the first page of a naturalization application. Follow the instructions on the form. If you are a U.S. citizen, practice filling out parts A and C only. If you are a permanent resident of the U.S. and plan to apply for citizenship, practice filling out parts A, B, and C. Also read Part 2. Do you understand the eligibility requirements?

OMB No. 1615-0052

N-400 Application
for Naturalization

Department of Homeland Security
U.S Citizenship and Immigration Services

Print clearly or type your answers using CAPITAL letters. Failure to print clearly may delay your application. Use black ink.

Part 1. Your Name. *(The Person Applying for Naturalization)*

Write your USCIS "A"- number here:
A

A. Your current legal name.

Family Name *(Last Name)*

Given Name *(First Name)*   Full Middle Name *(If applicable)*

For USCIS Use Only

Bar Code	Date Stamp

B. Your name **exactly** as it appears on your Permanent Resident Card.

Family Name *(Last Name)*

Given Name *(First Name)*   Full Middle Name *(If applicable)*

Remarks

C. If you have ever used other names, provide them below.

Family Name *(Last Name)*	Given Name *(First Name)*	Middle Name

D. Name change *(optional)*

Please read the Instructions before you decide whether to change your name.

1. Would you like to legally change your name? ☐ Yes   ☐ No

2. If "Yes," print the new name you would like to use. Do not use initials or abbreviations when writing your new name.

Family Name *(Last Name)*

Given Name *(First Name)*   Full Middle Name

Action Block

Part 2. Information About Your Eligibility. *(Check Only One)*

I am at least 18 years old **AND**

A. ☐ I have been a Lawful Permanent Resident of the United States for at least five years.

B. ☐ I have been a Lawful Permanent Resident of the United States for at least three years, **and** I have been married to and living with the same U.S. citizen for the last three years, **and** my spouse has been a U.S. citizen for the last three years.

C. ☐ I am applying on the basis of qualifying military service.

D. ☐ Other *(Please explain)* _____

Form N-400 (Rev. 10/26/05)Y

Getting a U.S. Passport

U.S. citizens may apply for a U.S. passport. When you apply, you need to show proof of U.S. citizenship and proof of identity. You also need two recent, identical (exactly the same) small color photographs. There is an application fee.

You need to submit your passport application to an agent at an authorized passport acceptance facility. This might be a post office or a local clerk's office near you. The web page for the U.S. passport application tells you how to find the nearest facility. The address for the web site is listed in the Resources section at the back of this book.

PRACTICE

Fill in items 1–22 of the following passport application. Print using capital letters, and follow the instructions. Notice the word *STOP* before item 23. When you finish item 22, stop. You do not sign the form until the agent tells you to sign it.

U.S. Department of State
APPLICATION FOR A US PASSPORT

OMB APPROVAL NO. 1405-0004
EXPIRATION DATE: 08/31/2008
ESTIMATED BURDEN: 85 Minutes
(See Instruction Page 3)

WARNING: False statements made knowingly and willfully in passport applications, including affidavits or other supporting documents submitted therewith, are punishable by fine and/or imprisonment under provisions of 18 U.S.C. 1001, 18 U.S.C. 1542 and/or 18 U.S.C. 1621. Alteration or mutilation of a passport issued pursuant to this application is punishable by fine and/or imprisonment under the provisions of 18 U.S.C 1543. The use of a passport in violation of the restrictions contained therein or of the passport regulations is punishable by fine and/or imprisonment under 18 U.S.C. 1544. All statements and documents are subject to verification.

When completing this form, PRINT IN BLUE OR BLACK INK ONLY

☐ 5 Yr. ☐ 10 Yr. **Issue Date** _____

☐R ☐D ☐O ☐DP

End. # _____ Exp. _____

1. Name of Applicant

Last	Suffix (Jr., Sr., III)
First	Middle

2. Date of Birth *(mm-dd-yyyy)*

3. Sex ☐ M ☐ F	**4. Place of Birth** (City & State OR City & Country)	**5. Social Security Number** (See Federal Tax Law Notice on Instruction Page 3)	**6. Alien Registration No.** (If applicable)

DS 11 06 2005

7. Height Feet Inches	**8. Hair Color**	**9. Eye Color**	**10. Occupation**	**11. Employer**

12. E-Mail Address *(Optional)*

13. Mailing Address

Street/RFD# **OR** Post Office Box		Apartment #
City	State	ZIP Code
Country *(If outside the U.S.)*	In Care of *(If applicable)*	

Submit two recent, color photographs

2" x 2"   FROM 1" TO 1 3/8"   2" x 2"

14. Permanent Address or Residence (If same as mailing address write "Same As Above")

Street / RFD # *(DO NOT LIST P.O. BOX)*		Apartment #
City	State	ZIP Code

15. Home Telephone *(Include Area Code)*	**16. Business Telephone** *(Include Area Code)*
( )	( )

17. Have you ever applied for or been issued a U.S. passport? ☐ YES ☐ NO If yes, complete the remaining items in block #17 and submit most recent passport.

Name in which your most recent passport was issued.	Status of recent passport ☐ Submitted ☐ Stolen ☐ Lost ☐ Other _____
Most recent passport number.	Approximate date your most recent U.S. passport was issued or date *(mm-dd-yyyy)* you applied.

18. Travel Plans

Date of Trip *(mm-dd-yyyy)*	Length of Trip	Countries to be Visited

19. Have you ever been married? ☐ YES ☐ NO If yes, complete the remaining items in block #19

Spouse's or Former Spouse's Full Name	Is your spouse *(or former spouse)* a U.S. citizen? ☐ YES ☐ NO
Date of Birth *(mm-dd-yyyy)* Place of Birth Date of Most Recent Marriage	Widowed? ☐ Divorced? ☐ Give Date:

20. What other names have you used? *(Include name changes, maiden name, & former married names)*

1)	2)	3)	4)

DS-11

Page 1 of 2

NAME OF APPLICANT (Last, First, Middle)	Date of Birth (mm-dd-yyyy)

21. Parental Information

Mother's Maiden Name				Date of Birth	Place of Birth
Last	First		Middle		

Father's Name				Date of Birth	Place of Birth
Last	First		Middle		

Is your mother a U.S. citizen?	☐ YES ☐ NO	Is your father a U.S. citizen?	☐ YES ☐ NO

22. Emergency Contact - Provide the information of a person not traveling with you to be contacted in the event of an emergency.

Name		Street / RFD #
Apartment #	City	State	ZIP Code
Telephone ( )	E-Mail Address (Optional)	Relationship

STOP DO NOT SIGN APPLICATION UNTIL REQUESTED TO DO SO BY PERSON ADMINISTERING OATH.

23. Oath & Signature

I declare under penalty of perjury that I am a United States citizen (or non-citizen national) and have not, since acquiring United State citizenship (or U.S. nationality), performed any of the acts listed under "Acts or Conditions" on this application form (unless explanatory statement is attached). I declare under penalty that the statements made on this application are true and correct.

X _____
Applicant's Signature - age 14 and older

X _____
Mother's Legal Guardian's Signature (If identifying minor)

X _____
Father's Legal Guardian's Signature (If identifying minor)

Applicant's or Father's Identification Information

Type of Document   Issue Date _____
☐ Driver's License   Expiration Date _____
☐ Passport
☐ Military Identification   Place of Issue _____
☐ Other (Specify)

Name _____

ID Number _____

Mother's Identification Information

Type of Document   Issue Date _____
☐ Driver's License   Expiration Date _____
☐ Passport
☐ Military Identification   Place of Issue _____
☐ Other (Specify)

Name _____

ID Number _____

FOR ACCEPTANCE AGENT USE ONLY

Facility Identification Number _____

☐ Acceptance Agent; Facility Name & Location

☐ (Vice) Consul USA; Location

☐ Passport Services Staff Agent

Subscribed & sworn to (affirmed) before me

_____ Date (mm-dd-yyyy) _____
(Signature of person authorized to accept application)

(SEAL)

For Issuing Office Use Only

Name as it appears on citizenship evidence _____

☐ Birth Certificate ☐ SR ☐ CR ☐ City File Date _____ Issue Date _____

☐ Passport Issue Date: _____

☐ Report of Birth ☐ 240 ☐ 545 ☐ 1350 Issue Date _____

☐ Naturalization Certificate Issue Date _____ Cert. # _____

☐ Citizenship Certificate Issue Date _____ Cert. # _____

☐ Other: _____

☐ Seen & Returned

☐ Attached _____

APPLICATION APPROVAL

FEE _____ EXEC. _____ EF _____ OTHER _____

DS-11

Page 2 of 2

Registering to Vote

If you are a U.S. citizen and are at least 18 years old, you can register to vote in the U.S. You register in the state where you live. Learn about and follow the rules for your state.

DMV Voter Registration

In some U.S. states, you can register at the DMV when you apply for a driver's license. When you get a driver's license, you show ID and proof of citizenship and write your name and address. You do not need to write that information again in order to register to vote. Read the basic requirements at the top of the DMV form. If you do not understand something on the voter registration form, ask for help.

Study the following voter registration form. These descriptions will help you fill it out for practice.

- Are you a U.S. citizen? To vote, you must be a U.S. citizen by birth or by naturalization. If you are a U.S. citizen, check *yes*. If you are not, you cannot vote in U.S. elections.

- Check any of the boxes that apply to you. You may check more than one. Are you registering to vote for the first time? Have you registered before but now you want to change information? Check the box(es) that describe the change(s) you need to make.

- The second line applies to changes. If this is a new registration, you do not need to fill in this line.

- Below the box, the form says "Choose a Party—Check one box only." There is a list of political parties. If you do not want to choose a party, check "I do not wish to enroll in a party." You check a box (join a political party) to vote in a **primary election** (an election to choose the candidate for a certain political party). Primary elections are held several months before a **general election** (an election to choose from candidates of different parties).

- **Affidavit:** Read these points very carefully and be sure you understand them. An affidavit is a sworn statement. You swear (promise) that you are telling the truth about the items listed.

- Signature: When the form is complete and you are sure the information is true, sign the application and write the date.

PRACTICE

Read this voter registration form that is part of a driver's license application. Then fill it out.

MV-44 (8/05)

NEW YORK STATE VOTER REGISTRATION APPLICATION

(Fill out this part <u>only</u> if you want to register to vote or change your address or other information with the Board of Elections, **and** if you are also filling out the DMV application on Pages 1 and 2.)

If you register to vote, your completed voter registration application will be sent directly to the Board of Elections. If you decline to register, your decision will remain confidential. You will be notified by your County Board of Elections when your voter registration application has been processed.

Are you a U.S. citizen? ☐ Yes ☐ No *If you answered NO, do not complete this form.*	I will be 18 years old on or before election day: ☐ Yes ☐ No *If you answered NO, do not complete this form, unless you will be 18 by the end of the year.*	Home Telephone Number (optional)
Last year voted	**Your Address was** (*give house number, street, and city*)	**In county/state**	**Under the name** (*if different from your name now*)

Choose a Party – Check one box only

☐ REPUBLICAN PARTY
☐ DEMOCRATIC PARTY
☐ INDEPENDENCE PARTY
☐ CONSERVATIVE PARTY
☐ WORKING FAMILIES PARTY

} *Please note:*
In order to vote in a **primary election,** you must be enrolled in a party.

☐ OTHER (write in) _____
☐ I DO NOT WISH TO ENROLL IN A PARTY

AFFIDAVIT: I swear or affirm that
● I am a citizen of the United States.
● I will have lived in the county, city, or village for at least 30 days before the election.
● I meet all requirements to register to vote in New York State.
● This is my signature or mark on the line below.
● The above information is true. I understand that if it is not true I can be convicted and fined up to $5,000 and/or jailed for up to four years.

↓   Signature or mark   ↓

X _____   Date _____

Separate Voter Registration

Many U.S. citizens register to vote by filling out a separate state voter registration form. The following is an example of a universal voter registration form that can be used in almost every state. Residents of New Hampshire and Wyoming should check with their town clerk or county clerk. North Dakota residents do not need to register.

PRACTICE

Fill out this state voter registration form. Items 6–8 may be optional in your state.

Voter Registration Application

Before completing this form, review the General, Application, and State specific instructions.

Are you a citizen of the United States of America? ☐ Yes ☐ No Will you be 18 years old on or before election day? ☐ Yes ☐ No **If you checked "No" in response to either of these questions, do not complete form.** (Please see state-specific instructions for rules regarding eligibility to register prior to age 18.)		This space for office use only.	

1	(Circle one) Mr. Mrs. Miss Ms.	Last Name	First Name	Middle Name(s)	(Circle one) Jr Sr II III IV

2	Home Address		Apt. or Lot #	City/Town	State	Zip Code

3	Address Where You Get Your Mail If Different From Above		City/Town	State	Zip Code

4	Date of Birth ___ / ___ / ___ Month Day Year	**5**	Telephone Number (optional)	**6**	ID Number - (See Item 6 in the instructions for your state)
7	Choice of Party (see item 7 in the instructions for your State)	**8**	Race or Ethnic Group (see item 8 in the instructions for your State)		

9	I have reviewed my state's instructions and I swear/affirm that: ■ I am a United States citizen ■ I meet the eligibility requirements of my state and subscribe to any oath required. ■ The information I have provided is true to the best of my knowledge under penalty of perjury. If I have provided false information, I may be fined, imprisoned, or (if not a U.S. citizen) deported from or refused entry to the United States.	Please sign full name (or put mark) ▲ Date: ___ / ___ / ___ Month Day Year

If you are registering to vote for the first time: please refer to the application instructions for information on submitting copies of valid identification documents with this form.

REVIEW & DISCUSS

Answer these questions. Talk to your classmates about your experiences.

1. What are the two ways someone becomes a U.S. citizen?

2. What does it mean to be a naturalized citizen?

3. Are you a naturalized citizen of the U.S.? If so, tell your classmates about the naturalization process and your citizenship ceremony (when you became a citizen).

4. When do you need a passport? Do you have a U.S. passport? Do you have a visa from another country? If so, tell your classmates about your experience when you applied for the passport or visa.

5. Talk about your experiences at U.S. Customs when you first entered the U.S. or when you returned from a trip.

6. Who can vote in the U.S.? Are you eligible to vote in the U.S.? Are you registered to vote?

7. What are the voter registration requirements in your state? Get a copy of the application form and discuss it.

© New Readers Press. All rights reserved.

Resources

Personal Information

For information about mail, postage, and zip codes, visit the U.S. Postal Service web site at www.usps.com.

The Change of Address form is available online at moversguide.usps.com.

For information about your state, visit the official state web site at www.state.[2-letter state abbreviation].US.

Banking and Money

Information on identity theft is available online at www.consumer.gov/idtheft/index.html.

Privacy: Tips for Protecting Your Personal Information is available online at www.ftc.gov/bcp/conline/pubs/alerts/privtipsalrt.htm.

Consumer Concerns

For free government publications and consumer information, visit the Federal Citizen Information Center web site at www.pueblo.gsa.gov/.

For consumer information and resources, visit the Federal Trade Commission's web site: First Gov for Consumers at www.consumer.gov.

Facts for consumers: Choosing and Using Credit Cards is available online at www.ftc.gov/bcp/conline/pubs/credit/choose.htm.

Education and Employment

For information about Social Security, visit the U.S. Social Security Administration web site at www.ssa.gov.

The SS-5 Application for a Social Security Card is available online at www.ssa.gov/online/ss-5.html.

For information about U.S. taxes, visit the U.S. Internal Revenue Service web site at www.irs.gov.

Internal Revenue Service Forms and Instructions are available online at www.irs.gov/formspubs/.

Health Insurance

For information about health care from the U.S. Department of Health & Human Services, visit the National Health Information Center's Healthfinder® at www.healthfinder.gov.

Driving and Automobile Insurance

For information about traveling safely with children in the car, read the National Highway Traffic Safety Administration's Traffic Safety Tips for Children, available online at www.nhtsa.dot.gov/people/injury/childps/newtips/index.htm.

Citizenship and Voting

For information about U.S. citizenship and immigration, visit the U.S. Citizenship and Immigration Services web site at: uscis.gov.

The N-400 Application for Naturalization is available online at: uscis.gov/graphics/formsfee/forms/n-400.htm.

For information about U.S. passports and international travel, visit the U.S. Department of State web site at: travel.state.gov.

The DS-11 Application for Passport is available online at: travel.state.gov/passport/forms/ds11/ds11_842.html.

For information on U.S. elections, visit the U.S. Election Assistance Commission web site at eac.gov.

The National Mail Voter Registration Form is available online at eac.gov/register_vote_forms.asp.

For information about the U.S. government, visit FirstGov.gov: The U.S. Government's Official Web Portal at www.firstgov.gov.